JOHN THOMAS
1838—1905
Photographer

HILARY WOOLLEN
and
ALISTAIR CRAWFORD

Gomer Press

770.9209429
woo

Printed and Published by
Gomer Press Llandysul Dyfed
with the support of The Welsh Arts Council

I SBN 0 85088 457 8

1519194

Contents

List of Plates

Where possible the titles are as given by John Thomas (where they appear on the negatives). Additional information has been used in some cases from details that appear on the paper envelopes containing the negatives. These titles are not attributed to John Thomas. In a few cases further information, such as date, has been added. The numbers after the titles refer to those given to the negatives by John Thomas, which are also used by the National Library of Wales for identification.

Acknowledgements

The authors wish to thank the National Library of
Wales, Aberystwyth for permission to reproduce the
plates from the John Thomas Collection and to extend
thanks to the staff of the Print Department for their help
and co-operation ; to Mrs. M. Carter, the University
College of Wales translator and Mrs. M. Denzey who
have translated from the Welsh ; to Mr. Llion
Williams of the North Wales Arts Association for the
loan of photographs from their collection ; to the
Welsh Arts Council for financial support without
which this publication would not have been possible ;
and to Mr. Peter Jones, Assistant Director, the Welsh
Arts Council, for his help and encouragement.

AC and HW   1977

Introduction

The discovery of the existence of a large collection of nineteenth century glass plate negatives of a Welsh photographer in the National Library of Wales stimulated the interest for this study. However, it was surprising to discover the lack of information concerning the life and work of the photographer, John Thomas (1838—1905). Despite the relatively early acquisition of the collection by the National Library in c.1920, and although many of his photographs have been anonymously used since then as illustrations, it seems not to have conjured up sufficient interest for anyone either to examine the entire collection in any great detail or for there to have appeared a published biography or complete catalogue; there is little more than a few articles. Although his name was very well known throughout Wales at one time there is the danger that his contribution not only to the social documentation of Wales in the late nineteenth century but also his place in the early history of photography will continue to be ignored and John Thomas as an individual will be forgotten. There are still a few Welsh people who are acquainted with his work but they have a scanty knowledge of him and of the subjects he photographed; curiosity had never motivated anyone to enquire further, in any depth until fairly recently. How far this can be attributed to the fact that he established his photographic business in and worked from Liverpool, rather than in Wales itself, is debatable. The more plausible reason is the reluctance to accept photography as a legitimate study. Nor did he achieve any measure of professional success in his own time. He seems to have had no connections either with the professional photographic circles operating in Liverpool, or the Liverpool Photographic Society, established in 1853, which has no record of his name. It also seems likely that his name was forgotten from the time of his death in 1905 until c.1920 when the collection of over 3000 glass negatives belonging to Sir Owen Morgan Edwards was handed into the keeping of the National Library of Wales. In 1928 it was the intention to publish a complete catalogue of the collection but alas this has still to be done.[1] There is a complete card index.

The knowledge of John Thomas and of the existence of his work did not in fact properly come to light until the late 1950's when the Honourable Society of Cymmrodorion first published the Welsh Bibliography. Dr. Emyr Wyn Jones was incensed with the fact that no Welsh doctors had been included. He was therefore asked to undertake some research work and to supply such information to the editor, Dr. R. T. Jenkins; and his request was eventually met by a supplement. Dr. Emyr Wyn Jones ventured into the details of the life of a prominent Welsh surgeon in Liverpool, a William Thelwall Thomas (the son of John Thomas) and was surprised to find that his father was perhaps a far more interesting subject than his son.[2] A fairly comprehensive sketch of John Thomas' history was published which made extensive use of various papers, letters and notes including many family papers lent by the grand daughter Mrs. Ifor H. Davies of Cerrigydrudion.

John Thomas' story is one of considerable interest as it reveals a man who devoted his life to a fairly prosperous business but was motivated by a sense of mission. The value of the collection lies not only in its existence as a social documentary of early Welsh life covering a wide range of architectural, topographical and social documentary subjects, but also as a 'complete' record of an early commercial photographer in the second half of the nineteenth century.

It is important to realise that in John Thomas' period photography was very much in its infancy; and he can therefore perhaps be seen along with other studio photographers such as Frank Meadow Sutcliffe 1853—1941 and Thomas Annan 1815—79 as making a personal contribution in this field. The fact that the collection is so extensive makes it of considerable importance in the history of photography.

In order to determine the aesthetic, documentary and technical merit of the photography of John Thomas, a biography is given and he has been placed, in this work, historically in relation to his contemporaries and to the position of photography both then and now. Arising out of this, the extent to which he can be credited with the title "aesthetic" photographer can also be considered along with the value of the photographs themselves. For a complete understanding of his work, some comprehension of the processing and technical developments involved in such early photography is also included.

However, there has been no attempt within this study to investigate the significance of his work in portraying the social history of Wales during the second half of the nineteenth century and no attempt has been made to catalogue or itemise the subjects. The plates have been chosen in relation to the text and have been selected primarily for their *photographic* considerations and in order to reflect the character of the travelling commercial photographer of the period. In so doing they also reflect the character of John Thomas himself and the conditions of his time, but much work remains to be done in this area and in cataloguing the complete collection. This must await a further publication. It is the hope that this study will place John Thomas in the context of the early history of photography and motivate further research and interest in the John Thomas Collection.

1. The Biography of John Thomas (1838—1905)

John Thomas of the "Cambrian Gallery" (the business which he established in Liverpool) was an early Welsh photographer who sought to capture and preserve many of the essential features of Welsh life and culture, during the second half of the nineteenth century.

Born in Glan-rhyd, Cellan in Cardiganshire on April 14th 1838, he was the son of David and Jane Thomas. Little is known about David Thomas except that he is described as a labourer on his son's marriage certificate and that he died on 3rd February, 1855. An account of his death is given in an emotional letter from Jane Thomas to her son who was by this time working in Liverpool.[3] His mother appears to have been fairly well educated, writing fluently in both English and Welsh, an unusual accomplishment in those days, which undoubtedly contributed considerably to his education. A photograph of her in Welsh costume is included in her son's reminiscences published in "Cymru" in 1898.[4] In this same article, there is a photograph of Glan-rhyd, his birth place, as it was in 1867, showing a cottage surrounded by trees, situated on the banks of the River Teifi; however, thirty years after John Thomas' departure in 1853, he was to find the garden overgrown and the old house reduced to rubble.

He received his early education in the village school at Cellan, where he also served as a pupil teacher prior to being apprenticed for a short period as a draper's assistant at Lampeter. In 1853, he decided to move to Liverpool, a three day journey in those days, northwards across rural Wales. The exact reason why he came to this decision is unknown, although in his memoirs[5] he relates how in anticipation he viewed the prospect through the rose-tinted spectacles of adolescence, but he admitted that he spent a sleepless night before his departure the following day, strengthened by family prayer and parental blessings. The details of the journey itself were also recounted in his memoirs; a night's rest in Tregaron with Dafydd Jones the egg-carrier and the next day, the long walk to Llanidloes. This involved a journey of some forty miles on foot through Pontrhydfendigaid, Devil's Bridge and over the shoulder of Plynlimon, where he described being knee-deep in snow on the 9th of May. The next day the two men travelled to Newtown, with an early start in order that Dafydd Jones would arrive in time for market. Here he caught the 'fly-boat' drawn by two horses, and in a few hours he had reached Rednal near Oswestry, where he could catch the Great Western for Liverpool.

For the next ten years he again worked in a Drapery Trading House, but the long hours and indoor work apparently undermined his health and before long he felt obliged to look for an open air occupation. He considered various types of employment and answered many advertisements, but finally became a 'Town Agent on commission' for a firm trading in writing materials and photographs of famous personalities. When he showed these photographs to his customers almost everyone asked him where the famous of Wales were. Only two notable Welshmen were included in the selection of the "Great Personalities of the World", they were two highly honoured men, the Bishop Short of St Asaph, and Sir Watkin Williams Wynn; one a cleric and the other a great landowner. Everyone mocked him saying that there were surely others apart from one bishop and a landowner. "I took the hint and considered whether it would be possible to include Wales as part of the world. And I felt the blood of Glyn Dŵr and Llywelyn[6] rising within me since I was jealous for my country and my nation at that time when its tide was only just on the turn". John Thomas was soon to realise the commercial potential for inclusion of Welshmen amongst the illustrious photographed personalities. It was this realisation which gave him the stimulus and motivation that set him on the new path of photography, which was to become his life's work. Photography in those days was not entirely regarded as a respectable trade but rather "the black art",[7] and according to Thomas' own testimony it had therefore fallen into the hands of "street vendors".

1

Having returned to Liverpool and gained a little insight as to how the firm he represented obtained the photographs which they published, he consulted several friends and suggested that maybe it would be possible to do the same for the famous of Wales and they encouraged him to proceed. His wife, however, was more antagonistic to the idea, afraid that he would turn into "an old man who took photographs a job which was looked down upon very much in the town. At that time the photographer would accost you on the street and try to get your order for a few pence and you could scarcely get past without having acceded to his request, but I took a broader view of the profession at that time." The latter remark was probably based on his respect for the "famous personalities" rather than on an awareness of the importance of photography. In the early days of photography, the mass of people were suspicious of the unusual powers of the new mechanism, not understanding the simple principles by which the process worked. Thomas had to battle with this prejudice against street photographers, but with such strong feelings about the position he thought he could establish for himself, he continued to overcome this barrier. At the beginning Thomas must have been ignorant of the theory and practice of photography.

Over the Whitsun of 1863 one of his friends was kind enough to accompany him to the house of the Deacon, Edward Morris, in Fraser Street, Liverpool, to be introduced to some preachers who were staying there. Having proposed his scheme to the ministers, he found that they were quite pleased with the idea especially when they understood that it would cost them nothing and that in addition Thomas intended to give each of them several copies of the photograph in return for permission to publish. It was in 1863 that he managed to acquire a camera and invite a number of these eminent Welsh preachers and ministers to have their photographs taken at his home. He saw the problem as "the bringing together of the Great Welshmen and the photographer". In each case "I had to ensure that the negatives were my own property, and I had to seek the permission of the photographed before publishing a picture".

To begin with, his first position was as Manager to Harry Emmens,[8] an eminent photographer of Seel Street, Liverpool; this lasted for two years, and Thomas' new Welsh business was handled through his employer and with his permission. However, in his employment with Harry Emmens, his responsibility was very limited; he found that he had nothing at all to do with taking the photographs, but only recording the names of the customers, looking after the details and sending the finished products to their homes. By 1867, he felt he had enough confidence and stamina to embark on a photographic business of his own, one which he intended to establish in Liverpool, but would be essentially a "Welsh business". He found pleasure in producing work of the highest quality, and as his business became more secure he employed experienced photographers to help him, particularly in the enormous task of processing and printing from the glass plate negatives at the Gallery in Liverpool. He took a house in St Anne Street and with his assistant, who was a skilled photographer working with him "I became what I am now", Thomas remarked, "an *Artist*. I had by this time added many new names to the list of Welsh notables and they still sold well". He had hoped at this stage that by taking many of the groups of the various Welsh denominations and also photographing the public generally, he would be able to provide a living for his wife, children and himself. Having mastered the technical aspects of the photographic processes, he advertised his business in the press and prepared classified lists of photographs that were available for purchase. He published a classified catalogue of the photographs available under titles such as bards, poets, musicians, singers, missionaries, church dignitaries and ministers of the Calvinistic Church of Wales. Besides these, he photographed rural scenes, ancient buildings, chapels and churches, characters and places of scenic beauty, on his various visits throughout Wales. In those early days many were

2

photographs of quite remote places, probably unphotographed until that time.

Having opened a picture gallery, the place attracted a great deal of attention from the various Welsh people who regularly visited Liverpool. "The Editor and old Patriarch Dd. Williams (Troedrhiwdalar) called in when on a visit to the town and both of them were very surprised indeed to see such a collection of Welsh people, old and new. 'This is indeed a Gallery' said the Editor, 'I must make reference to this on my journeys'. So also did Y Faner comment under the heading 'Here and there in Liverpool'. He asked me what I wanted to call the place, I said that I was thinking of Cambrian House. Cambrian House indeed, everyone will think that such a place sells cotton balls and pins, call it Cambrian Gallery, and such was its name for forty years".[9]

The year 1867 marks John Thomas' first visit to Wales in his new professional capacity, as a photographer, to photograph the Calvinistic Methodist Assembly at Llanidloes and in 1868 he visited the National Eisteddfod for the first time at Ruthin in Denbighshire and took photographs of the crowning of the bard. He visited these national events for thirty years so that he was able to produce a unique record of the national institutions of Wales from 1867—1900.

There are a few details of his family life, only that he married Elizabeth Hughes from Glandŵr, Bryneglwys, Denbighshire, the daughter of William Hughes, a joiner, in St Peter's Church, Everton on 23rd August, 1861 and it appears from the marriage certificate that she was nine years older than her husband. One can only assume from the wedding register that she was illiterate. When her husband left the security of the draper's shop to become a photographer, she greatly disapproved and resisted the change. In his biographical notes, Thomas attributes this to her naturally pessimistic nature; but within months, it seems her attitude had changed completely and she became an enthusiastic

saleswoman in his photographic business. Thereafter, she never made any disparaging observations about her husband's work and indeed her patient acquiescence in his long absences was essential for his work took him throughout Wales over long periods. She died in 1895, at the age of sixty-seven. Her brother, Thomas Glwysfryn Hughes, an enthusiastic Welshman, who was intensely interested in the culture of Wales, especially its music and literature and a member of the Gorsedd (the Bards that accompany the winner to be chaired at the National Eisteddfod) took over as an assistant and helped considerably in the business.

John Thomas' tenacity and enterprising attitude, his imagination and perseverance have left a store of information and insight not only into Welsh life, but into community life in the Victorian period. Thomas himself was aware of the historical value of his collection of glass plate negatives and consequently, in order to hand them down to posterity, he carefully selected over three thousand plates from his collection and sold them for "a very reasonable price" to Sir Owen Morgan Edwards[10] who used them to illustrate his many articles to depict Welsh life. Thus he secured the preservation of a choice selection dating from 1867 to the turn of the century. Sir O. M. Edwards on hearing of the death of John Thomas, in a letter to his son paid his respects to a great photographer and friend "his love for Wales and his keen interest in everything that related to Welsh life and literature and religion, made him one of the best friends I had. The readers of "Cymru" knew him well; he revealed himself unconsciously but thoroughly in his striking and readable articles".[11]

Interestingly, one of the most annoying features of any examination of a collection of photographs, particularly portraits, whether filed singly or in albums, is the lack of means of identifying the subject or persons presented, since too few people and even photographers took the time and trouble in recording names and dates

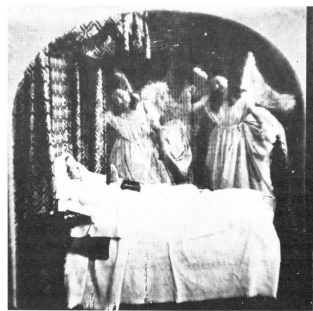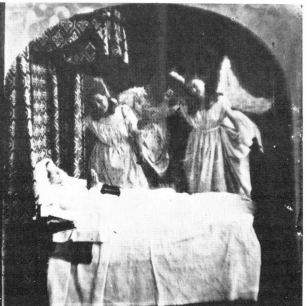

3

4

15

on the back of the plates. John Thomas, however, appears an exception, his great enthusiasm in his work and for his subjects led him to spend time meticulously marking and labelling each individual glass plate (rather than in an order book) with names, although unfortunately with very few dates.

It seems Thomas' interest was not completely confined to photography, he had a lively interest in antiques and in writing articles. He was a regular contributor to Welsh periodicals, especially editions of "Cymru". These articles described his travels and the people he met; they, like his seven personal notebooks, illustrate the remarkable insatiable appetite and dedication he had in his work. Among his published work, the writings of his early days in Cellan and Lampeter give an insight into the sincerity and poverty of the rural folk over a hundred years ago. He also contributed a number of articles to "Ymwelydd Misol" a monthly periodical published by the Calvinistic Methodist chapel in Fitzclarence Street and his account of the staunch characters amongst the old members of Rose Place Chapel is especially interesting, based as it was on his own personal knowledge and observation. Thomas was a religious man and he became a member of the Rose Place Chapel when he first came to Liverpool. On its closure in 1865 he joined the new Chapel in Fitzclarence Street where he and his wife remained members all their lives. Even though he was often absent from Liverpool, he would always go regularly to the Sunday services during his extensive journeys throughout Wales. This was essential to form patrons for his business and perhaps added to the respectability of the "street photographer" in otherwise hostile surroundings. The account of his early days at Cellan give a vivid insight into the life of rural Wales and his love of the country can be seen in the articles he wrote describing his outings to Dolgellau, Trawsfynydd, Llansannan, Ardudwy and Llangollen.

His dedication to his chosen mission and his love for his country which he felt deeply presumably helped him override the considerable difficulties in open air photography that were present at that time, since his use of the current photographic process, the wet-collodion system, involved long and complicated procedures. These difficulties of provision of adequate transport in some of the remote areas hindered the speed at which he could work, and this often proved a frustrating problem in itself where there only existed rough footpaths. Furthermore, transportation of the fragile plates back to Liverpool for printing and finishing, posed considerable problems.

Thomas died in 1905 in the house of his son Albert Ivor, and was buried in Anfield Cemetery, Liverpool. However, it seems, as far as can be traced, that his death did not lead to an obituary in the newspapers of the city.

The most prominent of his four children was William Thelwall (1865—1927) in whom Thomas' pride rested and who became an eminent surgeon and consultant at an early age, a lecturer in the medical department at Liverpool University, and eventually a Senior Consultant at the Royal Infirmary. He was the first surgeon in Liverpool to confine his work entirely to a consultative practice. It appears he was also very conscious of the essential Welsh background of his upbringing and seems to have retained an interest in Welsh affairs throughout his life. When he died in 1927 the appreciations in the press both local and professional were justifiably generous in praise of his brilliant attainments and career, but generally ignored what they perhaps regarded as his humble parentage. The other children were: Jane Claudia (1863—1934) who helped in his studio, Robert Arthur (1866—1932) and Albert Ivor (1870—1911) who also was a doctor. Yet it was the energy and persistence of the parents and in particular (considering the nature of Thomas' work) Mrs.

5

Thomas, which had made it possible to offer to their children many advantages which they themselves had not received. In his reminiscences, Thomas looked back on his career with this in mind:

"You will remember that I related many foolish things concerning vain dreams when I left home about making my fortune and lots of other things that will never come true as you can see from the beginning of this history of the Cambrian Gallery, many of the plans had become failures within the first ten years. But having got a foothold as it were I could see that the great inheritance had disappeared ever from my dreams, but I was determined on one thing, health and strength permitting, I would give the best education I could afford to my children, and if I couldn't succeed in that, to amass some money, houses and land to leave them something to quarrel and go to law about, my mind is quite easy that I have done something far better which is to give them an inheritance of the intellect rather than something in their pockets and let them fend for themselves".

Despite his own personal view of his failure, Thomas by his own diligence and fortitude had triumphed over many obstacles, in particular, the lack of formal education in his early days and ill health in his early manhood. He managed to combat many technical and physical difficulties with considerable skill in the performance of what had become a life's work. He systematically photographed his country with honesty and humanity and, in the end, achieved his fundamental ambition.

A reading of his memoirs which are essentially tales of characters he met, reveals Thomas as a man with a great love and respect for people, from whatever walk of life. At no time, in spite of some of the conditions he encountered, is there any tone of censure, except in the context of the national state. "But I dare to ask in the name of my country and my nation isn't there enough land in Wales to grow onions and many other things too? This country, and Wales also, pays thousands of pounds to foreign countries for them". Thomas, as has been said, considered himself as an artist and the work of taking photographs as an artistic experience. He was familiar, in particular, with the work of the topographical school of Turner, Cox, Moses Griffiths and appreciated their ability to translate the Welsh landscape. He had a simplistic view of art but, to an extent, an accurate one.

"No, before you may appreciate the picture you must go to see it with a heart that can feel or you might as well stay at home."

6

2.   The Photography of John Thomas

The very first men and women who took up photography usually owed their allegiance elsewhere, to other art forms. Many of the early photographers were artists. "The idea of elevating photography to the regions of Fine Art attracted chiefly former painters who found it easier to make a living with the camera than with the brush".[12] David Octavius Hill (1802-70), Oscar Rejlander (1813-75), William Lake Price (1810-96), Roger Fenton (1819-69), H. P. Robinson (1830-1901) and others followed, among them Julia Margaret Cameron (1815-79) a very exceptionally gifted amateur. These have now been recognised and to an extent documented. Yet alongside these leading photographers a commercial industry had grown up of studio photographers, some good, some bad, providing portrait photography for all. The majority of them were dependent on the saleability of their product in order to maintain a living.

John Thomas was one of the first men to take up photography from the beginning of his career. He belongs, as Michael Hiley described Frank Meadow Sutcliffe, a contemporary, "to the second generation of photographers, who took control of what had started out as a wonderful box of tricks which produced marvellous 'likenesses' and began to show what the camera could do in the hand of a man who devoted his whole life and creative energy to photography".[13]

John Thomas' chief importance lies in the fact that he was a photographer of an era and thus was able to make a fascinating record of the period in which he lived. He was also responsible during the forty years in which he worked for photographing every Welshman of note and virtually everything that came before the lens of his camera. He made photography a business and a profession and made a contribution to a truer understanding of late nineteenth century history. Although he began his work mainly stirred by the existence of few photographs of Welshmen, he did not concentrate on portraiture alone. His photographs are of both pictorial and human interest. Yet undoubtedly his range of subject matter was somewhat limited by the need for them to be of popular saleable topics. He still seemed able to encompass all manner of subjects from local characters, women in Welsh costume, morose Welsh ministers, scenic views, architectural subjects; including all classes, modes and ways of life in Wales. It must also be observed that many of his photographs could not be thought of as "saleable". His interest in documentation, at times, must have taken precedence.

The collection itself which covers the forty years from between the 1860's to the late 1890's is roughly catalogued under subject matter and filed in wooden boxes. Unfortunately, few of the glass plate negatives are dated, many are in poor condition and a few have shattered in their boxes. There exists a wealth of interesting notes and instructions scribbled on the margins of the plates, presumably intended for the attention of his photographic assistants, who furthered processing of the plates when they arrived at the Cambrian Gallery in Liverpool.

Although Thomas' memoirs are not strictly autobiographical, they are the best reflection of his character that can be found. The details reveal how John Thomas went about his work as a photographer, his opinions on every subject provide a unique insight into the attitudes of a business photographer in the late Victorian period. The immediate and personal nature of the notes can be judged by his identification with the reader and the constant use of rhetorical questions. The mass of information, incidental details, and personal reminiscences which have been preserved in his notes, have provided much of the material for this study. John Thomas remembers the first three men that sat for him at his home: the Reverend Hugh Jones of Llanerchymedd, Anglesey, the Reverend Owen Jones from Shrewsbury, later Bootle, and the Reverend A. J. Symonds from Fishguard and soon afterwards others were added. His work was first mentioned in "Y Faner" and then

7

8

21

in other Welsh papers. In John Thomas' words the response to his first few available photographs was encouraging. "The Press and periodicals in Wales gave a good coverage and publicity to my venture and the orders came rolling in". At the same time he was able to add to the list so that by the occasion of his second visit to North Wales he had the portraits of various famous Welsh people to offer to the shops and since these were being printed wholesale in Birmingham, it did not interfere with his assignments for the other Company, because his wages depended upon the number of orders he solicited. He concentrated more on the Welsh aspect and so the venture was a success. For the press he prepared classified lists of available photographs. Such a brochure set forth details of the notabilities in various groups; Bards, Musicians, Missionaries, Church Dignitaries and Non-Conformist Ministers.

When Thomas was manager in Mr. Emmens' establishment he made an agreement with him to take the negatives so that he was in a position to see that they were being photographed in the best possible way and he had an opportunity to talk to some of the people concerned. This is evident from the various places and people he met on his journeys. He intended the tales in his journals as additional notes to accompany the photographs, as a word of explanation of who they were.

Photography was still very much in its infancy and was therefore still a curiosity, and a novelty, especially for many of those in the working classes who were now able to buy a photograph of some well-known Welshman or perhaps even a relative. Thomas describes a visit to Llanuwchllyn in 1873 where he photographed men and women in costume, including many old preachers and deacons, many of these for the first time in their lives. He explained how he had "to coax and reassure many of them that his intentions were perfectly harmless". These portraits represent a large proportion of the collection. The subjects, mainly national figures (especially in religious and literary circles), local celebrities and characters, he has captured in a straightforward professional manner. He had begun by designing Commemorative cards (Cartes de Visite in Memoriam) of the old Welsh fathers, putting the name, date of their death and their age at the bottom and he found these most saleable products. "One I designed for the Rev. J. Phillips. I sold over one thousand of these in six weeks". Humorously John Thomas remarked "Trade depended on the popularity of the deceased". He seems to have favoured group portraits, the sixty-five Methodist ministers being the most wellknown of them, and from which possibly engravings were made, as in a similar composition of twenty-five Independent ministers of Liverpool (Plate 5). He used this technique widely, each miniature photograph (either a bust or a full-length portrait) taken separately and collectively mounted. Several of the early studio portraits of individual ministers appear to be taken in a very formal style. Thomas adopted a conventional composition; the figures rigidly seated, positioned to the left of a draped curtain and with the odd additional ornaments. Most of the ministers were photographed in the working apparel of the time, a black frock coat, and white tie or scarf tied in a bow, often holding a book, a form that was quite popular (Plate 7). In the carte-de-visite photographs,[14] men often posed leaning against Corinthian pillars or sitting on them, with a heavy curtain concealing the stand of the head rest. The photographer's studio became a stage with interchangeable properties and backgrounds in which the sitter became a figure in a landscape or background. However incongruous some of these pictures may seem, all these accessories have been borrowed from painting, in particular Van Dyck. It was partially ignored at this time that individuality is expressed as much by the figure as by the features, and that a portrait has much more character when the subject is in a position natural to him than when forced into one which he is unaccustomed to. Yet such was the trend of the fashion that people were frequently represented in

9

positions and in surroundings altogether unlike those in which their friends usually saw them.[15] Thus the general run of photographers were constantly searching for novelties in presentation to attract new clients and obtain fresh sittings from old ones. Each decade in the "carte" period was typified by some fashionable accessory. In the sixties the balustrade, column and curtain were ubiquitous. In the seventies rustic bridges and stiles were popular. The portrait of the Rev. L. Hughes posed against a painted backcloth of a mock Renaissance background is an excellent illustration of this (Plate 8), as is one of the gravedigger Dick Nancy standing comically tools in hand, against an interior window setting.

Obviously Thomas' prime concern was for an accurate recording of these Welshmen. Many hundreds are straightforwardly recorded, yet a progression can be traced, since later attempts seem a little less formal and the poses are more relaxed. In several portraits he has dispensed with a background, consequently such a finer simpler technique places greater emphasis on the silhouetted form of the minister. Gradually the portraits become more simple and honest and reflect greater depth of character.

No more truthful a representation of the period exists as of these ministers of the various denominations and the portrayal of rural folk. One is given an insight into nineteenth century rural life in Wales; the inaccessibility and isolation of the villages and towns (which governed the local pattern of life so much), the wide renown of certain local characters and figures and the striking poverty, narrow-mindedness and dignity of the Welsh people at that time. His love for Wales is reflected in the numerous stories and incidents that he retells and also in his photographic portrayals of the rural folk themselves. This section of his work illustrates his knowledge and appreciation of their background and environment. Thomas was continually reflecting his own humble Welsh origin.

On his travels throughout Wales, he passed from village to village seeking accommodation from the locals. His rate of work was also governed by their pace of life, as he was faced with difficulties of conveyance, and often forced to remain in one place for some time to await further transport. He saw a way of life even unfamiliar to himself. This is evident from his description of his visit to Machynlleth in 1870, "A quiet place with the inhabitants as if they were dozing if not fully asleep, you could stand near the Old Hall, where the Town Clock is now and look towards the South, East and the West on many a day without seeing a living soul except for the occasional dog greeting you or fighting with his fellow-creature".

In the hilly regions around Corwen he met and visited several interesting characters in their workshops and took many photographs, "I visited the cobbler in his workshop, the miller in his mill, the tailor, the post-master, the school-master, the butcher, the carpenter, the policeman and the publican. Each village had a sprinkling of craftsmen". This group of photographs is by far the most fascinating and revealing of those of the entire collection. He has captured with sincerity these individuals in natural, and excellent photographic poses, in their work clothes, holding the tools of their trade to represent their crafts (Plates 27 to 32). They are depicted without sentiment and remain free from nostalgia. The detail of these photographs is remarkable, as illustrated in the clarity of the slouched sleeping workmen on the bank, to which he jestingly added the caption "The Sleeping Beauties" (Plate 36).

The photograph he hung in the entrance to his Gallery depicted an old beggar woman of the name of Pegi Llwyd (Plate 12), one he came across in the Vale of Llangollen which harboured all sorts of persons; poets, authors and artists and this very strange character, a crafty wise beggar woman.

"Her business suit consisted of a short petticoat with several pieces missing at the bottom thus forming a sort of fringe, several unnecessary patches of different material for effect,

24

10

25

a short stick in her hand, an old basket on her arm with two handles, one of a piece of cane, and the other of leather. A little hat on her head with a patch on it of another colour with a hole in it and sometimes some of her hair poking through. You could see her often in front of the Hand Hotel and other large houses loitering around until she heard the sound of money coming down from the spectators at the windows. By a bit of persuasion and cunning, I took her photograph and when she found out that it was in a frame by the Gallery door, I almost felt the weight of the stick she carried, but as things turned out it was all settled with a little money."

In the stereoscopic photograph she is posed against a classical garden scene.

An unusual and most original photograph of "A Starved Boy" (misnamed as it depicts a girl) is included in the collection, yet there seem to be no others of its kind (Plate 44). This bears perhaps some relation to the work of Doctor Barnardo who set up a Photographic Department from 1874 to 1905 and whose work was of a similar style. This department was to take over 55,000 photographs of the children who passed through his homes; the photographs mostly taken systematically when the children were admitted, are a moving record of a section of society which until that time, had been virtually ignored by the camera and because the subjects are unselected within that category, the photographs are unique. Dr. Barnardo began to commission photographers to produce "before" and "after" pictures of the waifs. For the early 1870's, Barnardo's enterprise was extremely far-sighted. Documentary or systematic record photography was not commonly undertaken although since the 1840's the police had occasionally used civilian photographers to record prisoners. The 1870's were to see the real foundation of record photography. After the Arbitration Court had ruled against Barnardo on one of the published photographs as being "artistic fiction", the pictures became more functional and fitted the role of identity photographs rather than propaganda.[16] Thomas' photograph however is a studio portrait, but it is

questionable as to whether he was trying to convey any particular message. The use of the figure in the background is both sinister and evocative but may not have been intentionally so. This seems to imply that the child was of particular visual or social interest to him, but perhaps it was a simple commissioned work.

Many of the more interesting compositions are unusual groupings, the Welsh women arranged around a spinning wheel displaying their home craft (Plate 39), skilled trades such as the Morax workers (Plate 37), a rural industry which has long disappeared from Wales, and the informal groups of cottages at Carno Mill (Plate 23) or the staged grouping at Cemaes on a dry river-bed which illustrates his strange imagination for this absurd yet fascinating composition (Plate 2), repeated again in Mr. Evans' Boat (Plate 1). Thomas humorously retells an incident which occurred on a visit to a Mr. Wynne's home, in order to take some views and groups of workmen building an extension to the mansion.

"Having arranged everyone in his place and put their tools in their hands, while I was getting the plate out of its dark place one of them (who had a meagre knowledge of photography) suggested that each one should hold his tool in his left hand so that it would appear as if they were holding them in their right hands in the picture . . . the group was taken and by the time the picture was finished behold each one was a Benjaminite."[17]

In an isolated village called Ysbyty Ifan he found twelve almshouses, six for men and six for women; these were rent free and he photographed their occupants, "There was not a shop within eight miles; once a week, on a Tuesday, a carrier went to Llanrwst and took orders from the villages to replenish their essential food stocks". Here Thomas was able to describe a way of life unfamiliar to himself, and a place in which he felt as alien when he left as when he had arrived (Plate 42).

Thomas found pleasure in reconstructing scenes. His

11

12

arrangement of the stereoscopic drawing room scene in which the family are seated around the elderly reader (Plate 4) illustrates his interest in this popular form of photography with its unusual qualities of depth, which was particularly suitable for interiors. Despite his interest in the stereoscopic photograph, most of his attempts are not entirely successful. Between the years 1875 and 1876 he was asked to compose a photograph to depict the well-known story of Mary Jones who walked from Dolgellau to Bala to ask Thomas Charles for a Welsh Bible. "I was helped to find a model by a man named Mr. Rees, who searched the town of Dolgellau and surrounding country for a suitable sitter . . . he succeeded in part though not wholly. He liked the girl very much, although the old woman he was not fully satisfied with —I can almost see him now having put down the book, standing a little to one side with a satisfied smile on his face while I took the photograph". John Thomas speaks of the attempts of this same Mr. Rees to persuade him to take photographs of the town and country, yet he often disapproved "too many bricks and mortar" were his remarks, "seek for nature in the wild-life, the water-fall, that spring, the Torrent Walk, nature in the Wild". "It was easy for him to talk", as Thomas commented, "doing the job was the difficulty".

Landscape photography was by far more difficult and only the most enthusiastic photographer would embark on such. The difficulties of conveyance of the necessary equipment to isolated regions along rough tracks, in all weathers, were added problems to the laborious photographic processing of the wet-collodion system. The photographer may patiently wait for hours, only to achieve from a day's work one successful plate. Francis Frith (1822-98), a leading landscape photographer of the Collodion Period, spoke of the difficulties of getting a successful landscape. "Very rarely does a landscape arrange itself upon his focussing glass as well, as effectively as he could arrange it, if he could", wrote Frith.[18] The sensitivity of the wet-plate process however was ideal

for landscapes and architectural subjects where fine detail was needed (Plate 24). It was with these photographs he most extensively experimented blacking out areas, vignetting,[19] touching up[20] combining negatives, and erasing figures to correct compositions. It was the fashion at this time for the landscape photographer to go to great lengths to procure the best composition. Consequently for some, this involved transplanting trees, arranging the foreground with shrubs and branches and the tasks of a gardener. John Thomas did not use such extensive practices and many of the photographs are a true image of the life of rural Wales during his life time. His photographs of churches and chapels of every denomination, the houses of notabilities, ancient buildings and monuments are extensive, yet each seems to have had some significance for their inclusion in the collection. These, photographed in a variety of interesting ways, illustrate the dedication which governed his work perhaps to the point of photographing everything that was of *vague* interest and that he considered might possibly be saleable as prints.

His photographs are of both documentary and aesthetic merit and do not portray technical skill alone, although it cannot be disputed that he had mastered technique. Any systematic assessment of his work is very much a matter of conjecture, because there exist so few dates on the plates by which any development can be traced. Some of his photographic compositions appear to bear artistic qualities, but there still lies the possibility that he was relatively indiscriminate both in his choice of subject matter and in his use of composition. As Francis Frith again realised, paintings which photographers attempted to emulate were just vain dreams. "No man is so painfully conscious as he is that Nature's lights and shades are generally woefully patchy and ineffective compared with Turner's; and in short that although his chemical knowledge be perfectly adequate and his manipulation faultless, it is a marvel, an accident, a chance in a thousand when a picture turns out as

13

14

artistic in every respect as his cultivated taste could wish".[21] Conversely, the character of Thomas' work may be unique, because it was not governed by the photographic conventions of the time, of which he appears to have been largely unaware. Undoubtedly, the demands of a successful business to produce and sell as much as possible, since it was his means of livelihood, were generally antagonistic to creative self-indulgent work. In this sense perhaps John Thomas still did not live up to his own capabilities and potential.

15

31

The Technical Developments and Processes of Photography

The invention of photography was the result of various scientific and technical developments. Its evolution can be seen in several fairly distinct phases determined by the appearance of various new and improved techniques. The social effects of each of these major photographic developments were of significant importance. Although the wet-collodion process is of the most direct relevance in this study, since it was the main photographic process John Thomas used; some understanding of its position in the evolution of photography is desirable. Some photographic historians see a pre-snapshot age when a division appeared between those concerned with photography's social standing in relation to other fine arts, realising photography as an independent art medium, and those who were more largely concerned with the advance of the technical aspects of the actual processes of photography.

The invention of photography is largely restricted to the nineteenth century. The very first people to attempt to fix the images of the "camera obscura" were the brothers Joseph Nicéphore Niépce and Claude Niépce, officers in the French army and navy respectively, while stationed at Cagliari in Sardinia in 1793. The "world's first successful photograph" does not appear however till 1826 and was taken by Nicéphore Niépce who began experimenting in 1816 with pewter plates. He used bitumen of Judea as his sensitive substance, a compound which hardens when exposed to light. He thus obtained a faint "heliograph" or "sun drawing", the exposure lasting eight hours in full sunshine. The first recorded attempts to produce photographic images were made by Thomas Wedgwood at the end of the eighteenth century, using silver salts he was able to produce visible images by placing objects upon sensitised material. However he was unable to fix these images.

In 1829 Niépce signed a partnership agreement with Louis Jacques Mandé Daguerre, a theatrical designer and co-inventor with Charles Bouton of the Diorama. Two years after Niépce's death, Daguerre discovered that an almost invisible or latent image could be brought out or developed with mercury vapour, thus reducing the exposure time from at least eight hours to twenty or thirty minutes. It was not until 1837 however, that he found a means of fixing the picture with a solution of salt. Believing this positive process to be distinct from that of Niépce (though founded to a large extent on his late partner's knowledge), Daguerre called it the "Daguerreotypie". An era of the daguerrotype followed, although it was not until 1839, the official birthday of photography, that details of this first practical method of photography were revealed by Arago in France. It was from this date that miniature painters and engravers feared their livelihood, whilst Paris was filled with a mixture of bewilderment, excitement and disapproval—the whole of Paris was filled with "daguerreotypomania".

The only process that eventually established itself to some extent as a rival to the daguerreotype was the Calotype, the new improved version of "Photogenic Drawing", invented by William Henry Fox Talbot (1800—1877), an English landowner, scholar and scientist. After much experiment, in 1840 he discovered the possibility of developing the latent image, formed during a short exposure, with gallic acid (the action of the latter had been discovered independently by a scientist the Rev. J. B. Reade). The developed image on calotype paper was the exact reverse, as far as light and shade were concerned, of the original image. Such a picture was termed by Sir J. W. F. Herschel in 1841 a "negative", which was fixed with potassium bromide and later with sodium thiosulphate. The transparency of paper could be increased by waxing or oiling, and so Talbot was able to obtain true copies or positives of any negative by simple contact printing upon another piece of sensitised paper. Talbot patented this improved process which he called the Calotype on 8th February

16

1841. Later it also became known as the Talbotype. Talbot's process had now reached the same speed as Daguerre's had with chemical acceleration and offered the great advantage that any number of positive prints could be made. In this respect, it would be true to say that Talbot invented the 'photograph'. It is this negative-positive principle on which modern photography is based, whereas the daguerreotype which produced a single picture was a "cul-de-sac" in photography and inevitably disappeared.

Development of the negative-positive process could be more fully realised when a transparent support was found for the sensitive salts. Herschel suggested the use of glass plates, although glass had previously been used as early as 1822 by Niépce for heliography. Unlike paper it was not absorbent and so a suitable coating had to be found. Glass did take an image with much greater sharpness than the paper used by Talbot. In 1848 the Albumen process emerged, when Abel Niépce de Saint-Victor (a couson of Nicéphore Niépce) suggested its use as a vehicle for silver iodide. It was the first practical method of photography on glass. The cheapness of the albumen and its transparency made it a perfect base for the multiplication of copies, and but for its fragility and weight, no doubt it would have established itself as an ideal carrier of photographic emulsions. However the Albumen process was slow, requiring a long exposure of between five and ten minutes. This length of exposure time continued to hinder other photographic developments. Although for portraiture it proved rather inadequate, it was ideal for landscapes, architecture and art reproductions. The exposure could be considerably reduced if the plates were exposed immediately after sensitising and whilst still moist, but this entailed the burdensome haulage everywhere of a darkroom and chemicals. On the other hand the prepared plates could be kept for a fortnight and development postponed for a week or two. The process itself, which produced prints of very fine detail, was in use until 1851, when Scott Archer published his wet collodion process.

1851, the year of Daguerre's death[22] also marks the beginnings of a totally new period in photography, with the invention of Frederick Scott Archer's wet collodion process. The relaxation of Talbot's[23] patent in 1854 and the almost simultaneous perfection of the collodion process made photography at last a really popular pursuit. The daguerreotype patent had also run its term by 1853, so now all the photographic processes were available to anyone amateur or professional. "No longer was photography an art for the privileged, it had become an art for the million".[24] This collodion process provided a great impetus to the general expansion of photography not only in the field of amateurs, but also its emergence as an industry. With mistaken ideas as to the ease of the new method, large numbers of amateurs purchased the necessary equipment. Consequently, with the popularisation of the art as a result of the new process, not only were there thousands of new-comers, but there soon arose an insatiable demand for photographs of all kinds of subjects.

The census returns of 1841 and 1861 give some idea of the vast growth of photography during these twenty years. In the census of 1841, photography does not appear as a profession, ten years later only 51 photographers were recorded, yet in 1863 (a few years before Thomas entered the profession) it listed 2,534 photographers in Britain, 400 of them in just three principal cities in England and Scotland, and employing over 4,000 assistants. In 1851, a Miss Wigley was the only woman professional whilst ten years later there were 204. By 1861 two dozen photographic societies had been founded, which further publicised and encouraged interest. In 1841 there were three portrait establishments in London, in 1851 there were a dozen, in 1855 a rise to 66, in 1857 to 155, and in 1861 to over 200.[25] This rapid growth was due to a number of factors; the main processes were free of patents after 1853, the appearance of the new collodion process; and also stereoscopic photography which caught the public imagination.

17

The wet collodion process as it was called, used glass plate negatives which the photographer had to coat with silver salts in collodion. After exposing and before the coating had time to dry, the latent image was developed again by the photographer in order to produce the negative. These operations had to be carried out within a very short period of time as the coating quickly lost its sensitivity when dry. Despite all the encumbrances this involved, photographers rapidly took to the wet-collodion process, since it yielded negatives of high quality and detail and also, being sensitive, the exposure time was reduced to only a few minutes.

All the equipment necessary for this process, its weight and bulk, was too great an encumbrance for all but the most enthusiastic toughened and patient touring photographer. In addition to the camera and a sturdy tripod, the photographic tourist was supplied with a choice of several lenses, a chest full of chemicals and made-up solutions for coating, sensitising, developing and fixing the glass negatives, a number of dishes, a good supply of glass plates, scales, weights, glass measures, funnels and a pail to fetch the rinsing water. Above all he needed a portable dark tent in which all the chemical processes could take place. Those who thought it both ungentlemanly and uncomfortable beneath the weight of cumbersome apparatus, engaged a porter. In the photograph of Gwaith Sets, Llanaelhaiarn (Plate 26) we can just observe a tripod on the beach, a horse or pony near by and a cart with a large pack. Thomas seems unconcerned at photographing these objects as he viewed the landscape, but it does present a rare and interesting photograph of his travelling equipment and displays the problems involved. At a time when each photographer was, out of necessity, required to learn how to delicately manipulate chemicals and chemical apparatus, it is no wonder that the photographic journals of the day have so many descriptions of the new techniques developed by the enthusiastic amateurs, between 1839 and 1885.

The camera was able to reproduce with ease, images which academic painters were struggling over, but it also recorded the personal marks, characteristics and other features such as pockmarks, blemishes, ill-fitting and wrinkled clothes. Yet photography, in spite of the beautifying effect of retouching which developed, contradicted some of the stereotyped views of personality that existed and for the first time people were able to examine themselves in detail. They were also faced with a new form of portraiture, no longer just an indication of social standing. Unfortunately, it became the common complaint that the camera represented the countenance too truthfully, and soon the general practice was for photographers to correct this, by removing blemishes, and adding points of beauty lacking in nature, by very careful retouching, to satisfy the sitter. This soon led to codes of retouching.[26] As Gernsheim stated, "It may be legitimate to hide defects by skillful posing and clever lighting, but beautifying can only be done by a manual interference with the negative or print and the photographer then leaves his proper domain of drawing with light and becomes that curious hybrid, the painter-photographer".[27]

In the late 1850's retouching and beautifying were carried to such extremes that some photographic societies banned "coloured" photographs altogether from their exhibitions, and also in the case of touched-up photographs, often stipulating that the negative should be displayed alongside the print. Indeed the ease with which anyone with a little skill could either add to or take away from parts of the picture represented a dangerous temptation to photographers to give way to the sitter's desire for either a very flattering portrait or else to obtain "artistic" effects.

One of the most obvious ways in which the photograph distorts natural objects is its inaccuracy in translating colour into tone. The black and white plate was not sensitive to all colours, there were no means of distinguishing between certain combinations and of

18

course, no means of distinguishing the same tones produced by different colours. This is one of the fundamental problems that photography is faced with. The shapes of the forms which are only distinguishable because of their colours may be entirely lost. The very earliest photographic emulsions were as sensitive to blue as to white, for example, while both yellow and red objects were rendered quite dark, blues and violets were rendered quite light. Therefore one can imagine the difficulties facing portrait and landscape photographers before the 1880's, when orthochromatic plates became generally available. If measures were not taken one can well understand the chagrin of excessively ruddy-faced sitters when they were handed their likenesses. Not until the twentieth century was panchromatic film able to improve the tonal accuracy of the photograph and was able to conform more closely with optical perfection.

The photographing of clouds, particularly if the landscape was also to be included, was a very different matter and presented great problems. Different exposure times were necessary if both the expanse of light sky and the darker tones of the land were to be recorded correctly. In practice however, either the sky was over-exposed and the definitions of the cloud forms lost, or if the exposures were set for the sky, the terrestial forms would be under-exposed. Therefore, in the print, if exposed for the sky, the foreground became a silhouette, whilst if the exposure was set for the landscape, the sky was too dense and printed white and any clouds there may have been did not appear. The most obvious method proposed to circumvent the difficulty was that of taking separate pictures of the land and sky and placing the negatives together from which prints could then be made.[28] Another means of overcoming this was simply to black out the sky, so that it appeared uniformly white in the positive. However photographers soon found this unsatisfactory, and began dabbing artificial clouds on the negatives. Favourite cloud negatives were made to do duty for totally different subjects, sometimes

with startlingly incongruous results. Still more absurd was the fact that different photographers might be using the same cloud negative, for from 1880 onwards they became an article of commerce. Towards the end of the century complaints were still being made that photographs were being pieced together, composite landscapes with cloudy skies "taken at noon, above a quiet landscape taken in the morning or evening".[29]

Photographs of portraits and interiors can be found taken after the mid 1850's in which the violent contrast between dark and light masses literally eradicate any intermediate tones. This feature can be noticed in many of John Thomas' early portraits. In the photographic circles, many photographs of this kind were often considered to be failures because they did not have the quality that was in photography, the subtlety and transitions of tone ranging between black and white.

The collodion process was attractive because of its speed, although the plate had to be exposed and developed in a moist state. "Exposure was based on guesswork tempered by experience"[30]. If the coat was allowed to dry, the nitrate of silver crystallised and this spoiled the picture; also the pores of the collodion contracted and the developer could not penetrate it. The inconvenience of dark tents and other equipment, which had to accompany the photographic landscape tourist on his travels was so great that there soon arose a great desure for a "dry plate" or at least some means by which the collodion could be kept sensitive for an extended period of time. Therefore from the mid 1880's there appeared various emulsions which had the effect of preserving the collodion coating in a sensitive state for several days or even weeks, thus allowing the entire chemical manipulation to be carried out in the photographer's own darkroom at home. However, this lengthened the exposure time quite considerably and the preservative processes in themselves were complicated to manipulate, so the wet collodion process still remained the most favourable.

19

20

By 1885 the wet-collodion process was truly obsolete, and was now a thing of the past for all but "collodion" specialists, and photographers found their techniques had been revolutionised by a new successful dry-plate process. "The whole paraphernalia of the wet collodion process could be dispensed with. The snap-shot had arrived".[31] This alone was enough to drastically revolutionise photography and its place not only in the arts, but in society. Photography in the pre-snap shot age was mainly a matter for professionals and some of the best of them were former artists or had received some art training. It was with this disadvantage that John Thomas, having had no type of formal education entered the practice of photography and established his business.

It appears from the limited source material available that John Thomas used the camera as an instrument, a means of recording reality, yet undoubtedly with much professionalism in its handling. He also worked with some of the current techniques that were available, the wet and dry plate systems, and in particular stereoscopic photography. Apart from his studio portraits there is a distinct lack of any staging or use of devices during processing, indeed he does not appear to have been particularly concerned even with cropping.

New cameras were constantly appearing on the market, some of them for novelty alone. In the 1850's the stereoscopic camera was introduced, to enable two pictures of the same object to be taken from two slightly different viewpoints, giving an impression of relief and astonishing reality when viewed in a stereoscope. John Thomas worked with these stereoscopic devices. A number of his plates which can be clearly identified as "stereoscopic" cover a wide and fascinating range of miscellaneous subjects. It seems stereoscopic photography did not arouse public interest until Sir David Brewster's lenticular stereoscope had established itself, for the difficulty and cost of producing two large photographs for Wheatstone's reflecting stereoscope kept their price

high. (In 1832 Sir Charles Wheatstone had first noticed the strange phenomena and had worked on experimental optics.) In 1849 Sir David Brewster brought out a modification of the second-type of stereoscope suggested by Wheatsone in 1838, which was able to give "wonderful relief". When the collodion process had established itself, stereoscopic photography like photography in general received a tremendous impetus, for paper positives mounted on cardboard could be mass produced and sold at a fraction of the price of a stereoscopic daguerreotype. Yet with increasing popularity and its widespread use for all manner of things, a change of taste set in; the stereoscope became the poor man's picture gallery. Brewster, it seems, also bears the responsibility for "spirit photography", something which again John Thomas experimented with. The idea had occurred to Brewster in 1844 after seeing a calotype by Hill and Adamson in which a boy had seated himself during part of the exposure on one side of steps near a doorway and appeared transparent in the print. Consequently, as John Thomas found, allowing the figures to appear for just part of the exposure gave them a spiritual or ghostly appearance and seems to exhibit them as "thin air amid the solid realities of the stereoscopic picture" (Plate 3). The extreme popularity of stereoscopic pictures began quite early in the mid-fifties, and affected the whole of the so-called civilised world for fifteen years, as Helmut and Alison Gernsheim observed, it was claimed no home was without a stereoscope.

From his notes it appears that John Thomas favoured the wet-plate process and its sensitivity until the introduction of the "dry-plate" system. When first employed by Harry Emmens, the Liverpool photographer, the plates had to be sent to Birmingham to be processed and developed. When John Thomas had formed his own business the plates were transported from all parts of Wales to his gallery in Liverpool where they were processed.

Thomas speaks in his memoirs of the difficulties

21

22

involved in the use of the wet-plate process, and the considerable equipment necessary particularly if he wished to sell the photographs locally.

"He kept on persuading me to take photographs of scenes in the country and in the town. I did and when I showed them to him he said, 'Too many bricks and mortar here—this waterfall, that spring, the Torrent Walk, nature in the Wild—' it was easy for him to talk, doing the job was the difficulty. Under the old system to make a good trade out of Views one needed the proper provision, viz.—a sort of closed carriage or caravan on a small scale so that you could take all the chemicals with you and all the paraphernalia wherever you wished and then when you had got as close as you could to where you wanted to photograph you had everything you needed in the vehicle and all you needed was to draw the curtains over the windows and you had a Dark Room since by the Wet Process before the Dry Plate was invented it wasn't possible to keep the plate for more than ¼ hour after preparing it before one had to take the photograph and develop it and so you can see how difficult it was to go any distance to take a View or a Group and many times during my journeys in those first years I would like to have gone a few miles to take some pretty scene or some historically interesting place but I had to count the cost before setting out since I knew I couldn't the gain. It involved physical effort too; one had to have 5 bottles full of various chemicals, a heavy bath weighing about 6 lbs, glasses and cloths to make a dark place apart from the camera, the lenses and the stand—one needed the assistance of a man, a mule, a horse a vehicle or something to carry one for a little way. After arriving, search for somewhere suitable to convert into a dark room, get a pitcher or two of water to make sure of the picture, and then pack it all up and set out for home—the best part of the day if not all of it having been spent in getting perhaps just one photograph.

And perhaps I should mention the inconvenience of trying to find somewhere suitable for a Dark room, especially in the quarrying areas or on top of a mountain—places far from any house. I used many sorts of places for the purpose —a chicken coop, a stable many times, and once a cave when I took the group of Bards in Ruthin Eisteddfod but the darkest place I was ever in was an empty grave in Smithdown Lane Cemetery in Liverpool when taking a photograph of the grave of Rev Pearse, namely the father of Mrs. H. E. Thomas when they were about to leave Birkenhead for Pittsburg in America. When I reached the spot where the grave was, it happened to be very far from any house, even from the entrance and there was no cabin or shed in sight anywhere but nearby there was a half dug, empty grave with a ladder into it—and after some consideration and with the help of the assistant, I decided to go down into the grave and having got the bottles and other necessary items and arranged them at the bottom of the grave and having got a jug of water from some workmen nearby, and made everything ready my assistant put another ladder across the top and yellow curtains over it and that was how we developed the film. After climbing out I could say like Griffith Jones Tregarth that I had come from the grave, but not because I had gone there too soon after the announcement but because I had completed my work there."

However Thomas did not seem over-troubled by difficulties in his early ventures; the trials faced by every photographer. Sutcliffe recollected; "when we consider our work seriously . . . we cannot help wondering what attractions photography had for us when young, that we should give the rest of our lives to it. Certainly the prospect of having to stand in front of an evil-smelling sink, with our hands in poisonous chemicals, in a darkroom with a dimmed red light in our eyes, for the best part of every summer's day, did not enter into our youthful calculations."[32] Although Thomas does not directly mention changing to the use of dry plates, when they appeared on the market around 1880 one can assume this was so. In his notes he speaks of the years 1878 and 1879 when business was flourishing and pay day involved as many as ninety-five photographs in one day using the dry-plate system in order that the processing could be left until the following day.

23

4. The Art Photographer

During the 1840's before photography had properly established itself in Britain, there were many signs of a new interest in visual documentation particularly in pictorial satire. The most dramatic use of photography as reportage was not surprisingly in the context of war. For the Victorians, war was a distant activity and photography was one means by which it could be brought nearer to home. Roger Fenton was one whose photographic activity in the Crimea resulted in a large collection of war photographs that have since become famous. However, the photographs of the American Civil War by Mathew Brady (1823-96) in the 1860's were more horrifying and truthful. The very fact that these photographs are better known today than they ever were in the nineteenth century is in itself significant of the period. However it was not until the beginning of the twentieth century with the advent of the half-tone process that the photograph supplanted the engraving and became reportage photography that is now standard in our press. The essential elements of this tradition were laid by photographers such as Fenton, Beato, O'Sullivan (1840-82), etc. Social documentary photography is marked by the appearance of John Thomson (1837—1921) with his photographs of street life in London in 1877 and by Thomas Annan (1829-87) who photographed the slums of Glasgow in 1877. Social genre photography fascinated some of the art photographers and continues to do so and in any analysis of the period it should be remembered that depending on the individual photographer, these areas are frequently combined and overlap.

Roger Fry has questioned how far a period can be transmitted particularly in relation to the work of Julia Margaret Cameron,[33] obviously in the matter of the transmission of a period, photography is of immense importance. "It bears repeating that the photograph opens up an immense visual field. Natural conditions so transient that they would normally be beyond the reach of even the most skilled draughtsman working from memory; the unselective character of the lens; the fact that the images are accessible in the hand at any time, in a way that nature is not—these are among photography's exclusive characteristics. In addition, aspects of nature and of human situations otherwise completely lost in time past continue to exert their unique *cachet* through the photographic print. The frozen and remote feeling of an old portrait photograph which repelled artists like Redon has had an intense attraction for others. The subjects, even those in synthetically casual poses, have a rigid alertness that belies their awareness of the camera. Once considered too unnatural, this rigidity now has an appealing stylistic flavour."[34] This description is particularly echoed in the work of John Thomas.

A study of the social effects the various new discoveries in photography had on the society of the time is particularly useful in attempting to understand the nature of the photographic image. We should not forget, however, that for many photographers each new image was often incomprehensible. In the Victorian era, photography first made its impact on the world: by 1871 it was observed as "the greatest boon that has been conferred on the poorer classes in later years".[35] Even in the nineteenth century, the social effects of photography were commented upon. "Photography helps develop the idealistic capabilities of the masses, social affections are enhanced increasing the knowledge and happiness of the masses".[36] Above all no longer was photography an art for the privileged few, but the photographic album became the portrait gallery of the middle class, the postcard the photograph for all. G. M. Trevelyan in his much renowned volumes on English Social History also acknowledges the importance of photography by his inclusion of part of an article from The Photographic News. "Photographic portraiture is the best feature of the fine arts for the million that the ingenuity of man has yet devised. It has in this sense swept away many of the illiberal distinctions of rank and wealth, so that the poor man who possesses but a few shillings can command as perfect a lifelike portrait of his wife and child as Sir Thomas Lawrence

24

painted for the most distinguished sovereigns of Europe".[37] Instead of the laborious painted portrait, often in miniature, and certainly executed in the tradition of portrait painting, the photography, with its ease of execution, and in many cases, its more accurate representation, became the obvious substitute. This visual record of identity and proof of existence at a specific time has continued to fascinate the majority to this day. Most amateur snap-shots are in fact of people, more often than not, known to the photographer. This love of the portrait is more than mere vanity and would appear to be psychologically important for various reasons. In many ways there was attempted a straight transference from the portrait painting to the photograph and the conventions of painting were imitated. Provided these conventions were maintained, the public seemed unconcerned with any lack of interpretation or insight.

The invention and increasing popularity of photography, however, was a direct threat to the Fine Arts; artists felt their positions dangerously challenged by this new invention which was able to represent more accurately and with little skill what second-rate artists had difficulty in drawing, and from the moment it was introduced in 1831, painters regarded this scientific marvel with suspicion. The effect of each photographic development can be mirrored in the reaction of artists and reflected in the Fine Arts of the period. Lady Eastlake, the wife of Sir Charles Eastlake, who was the director of the National Gallery in 1855, observed that the new invention fell between known categories, "neither the province of art, nor description but of a new form of communication between man and man, neither letter, message nor picture, which now happily fills the space between them."[38] Yet the distinctions between art and photography in portraiture were to be far more confused than her description suggests.

As Tristram Powell stated unfortunately "the camera could reproduce with ease images which academic painters struggled over".[39] The daguerreotype photograph provided a fairly cheap, accurate and quickly produced substitute for the miniature portrait which for a period was forced into oblivion and eventually extinguished. Although sitters did not always feel flattered by the results, they were looking at the first unique mechanical likenesses of themselves. It was from this photographic achievement that confusion in the Arts arose and the subsequent questioning of the respective roles of all areas of the Fine Arts. By the 1850's, one can safely say portrait photography had almost completely supplanted miniature painting and in 1859 for the first time, not one miniature was shown at the Royal Academy Exhibition.

In the first decade, following the introduction of photography, painting and drawing styles became noticeably more tonal and photographic. At first it was thought that the photographic image might be the standard against which all representational and naturalistic painting could aspire to and be measured by. However, it was not long before it became quite obvious that there was no uniformity in the images produced by the camera; not only because of the technical difficulties that occurred in the photographic processes, but also because these processes were subject to factors other than simply mechanical control. Continually there were attempts to relate "photography" to one or other theory and to view it as a simple visual system. The complexity of the photographic language was not at first sight acknowledged and indeed is only now becoming more apparent. This simplification of definition continued to produce arguments that either favoured photography as art, or merely as a recording device. Initially artists (especially the portrait painters) began to use freely and openly the photograph as an aid, enabling them to dispense with sketches and studies from models. The progression of this use of photography and the eventual analysis of its characteristics, both intentional and unintentional, for example the blurred image, the new viewpoint

25

and perspective, the photographic use of tone, the viewfinder rectangle and the arbitrary composition, led logically to Impressionism. The mechanical device which gave to the world for the first time realistic representations of any subject matter ironically led artists to totally abstract art and to an investigation of aesthetics *per se*. The use of photography as an aid, however, inevitably leads to the representation not of the subject matter depicted, but of the photograph itself, unless deliberately bypassed or altered. The obviousness of this factor seemed to escape the artist's and the public's observation and many were to use photographs surreptitiously. Reality in many respects became photographic reality.

Conscious of the rigid mechanical limitations of their medium, photographers increasingly poured their energy and skills into developing new, often elaborate means of augmenting the artistic content of their work to the point of attempting to imitate painting. Their aggressiveness grew, and they saw little reason why photography should not be seen as a "fine art" and thus share the advantages enjoyed by both painting and sculpture and perhaps of more importance, share the status of "artist". The Art Journal in 1862 published a note of the Photographic Society's complaint that the Commissioners of the International Exhibition held in England had denied photography the right to take a place amongst the Fine Arts, and had placed it with carpenters' tools and agricultural implements. Painters were accused of copying photographs while photographers were ridiculed for styling themselves as "artist photographers" and for making absurdly high artistic claims for their work. As the influence of the photographic image spread to all spheres of art, anxiety about the growing photographic style in painting increased and within twenty years of its appearance, it was seen as a pernicious influence over art. "By invading the territories of art this industry has become art's most mortal enemy. If photography is allowed to supplement art in some of its functions, it will soon have supplanted it or corrupted it

altogether".[40] Photography was seen as having a beneficial, even purgative effect on painting. It was recognised that photography had swept away third and fourth rate painters and turned them into photographic colourists. This however, was also unfortunate for photography, for it was these third rate artists who, in abandoning painting in favour of photography which they claimed was equally an art (which also held out greater prospects and proved more lucrative) brought to photography misconceived notions of its proper functions. Misconceptions which still persist. The photograph, on the other hand, forced its own representation of reality to the point where its truth became accepted as *the* truth. The photograph did become and to an extent still is, the standard by which reality is measured. This was to revolutionise art. It was pointed out that the daguerreotype demonstrated correct aerial perspective by showing that the brightest parts of a view were on the foreground and not in the clouds or in other parts of the sky as had been thought to be the case by artists. However, although printmakers, artists and sculptors readily accepted the aids of photography, or else used them as their primary source for portraiture, they usually made alterations which were considered in their eyes to be improvements on the camera likeness. Even so one cannot fail to notice that distinct traces of the appearance of a sitter's face taken from photographs were retained in oil paintings. At the Royal Academy, the artists took the appearance of photography in their stride, acknowledging its emergence, but in no way believing their positions to be truly challenged. Poynter, who succeeded Leighton as Principal of the Royal Academy in 1896, claimed in 1879 that "he believed photographs were of a certain value in preliminary studies, but in finishing the artist should go it alone". The 1870's had produced, he complained, "those poor substitutes for photographs in the shape of elaborate studies from nature which some of our modern artists give us under the name of realism . . ."[41]

Threats of the possibility of colour photography arose.

26

49

T. F. Goodall a landscape painter and photographer, was quoted to have said, "when photography can be taken in natural colour, then will be the time to discuss the dying groans of painting".[42] Others viewed the possible arrival of colour photography more sensibly as did August Pointelin in 1908. "I believe that photography having finally become practical will rid painting of all the detectable and finicky daubers who know nothing of nor understand nature".[43] From the 1860's and 1870's, colour photography was imminent and it seemed photography might take possession of all pictorial representation. It therefore became necessary for the revival of more spiritual values in art; a return to art's higher realms had to be fostered. The artist was driven to take refuge more and more in theory, and in a series of intellectualised experiments in "Art for Art's Sake". Because of the stigma attached to artists who were known to rely on photography, its use was generally concealed so that many photographs were hidden or destroyed afterwards.

As Sutcliffe realised, compared with painting, photography allowed anyone who could master the process to make detailed representations of views in a very short time. "The weak point of photography is that except in the hands of anyone who has been trained from infancy to see, it 'draws' too much, and the eye is vexed at having to reject so much".[44] The nature of the activity, chemical and technical, did not require the same talents as the ability to draw or paint. This dichotomy still poses problems today in relation to the training of photographers. With the invention of photography, the non-artist was able for the first time to express and produce art works. Part of the prejudice that surrounded photography then, and even now, has stemmed from the artist's, and via the artist, the public's inability to accept that the talents and knowledge required for the painting are not necessarily similar to that required for the photograph. In the early period this was even more so when the photographer had to be his own processer and printer.

For photography to be considered truly as an art form, it became necessary to settle the question of whether or not it was possible to manipulate the medium in the way that a painter is able to, and therefore whether photography could be described as artistic. It was over this fundamental concern that a schism developed, as a result of those who wished to elevate photography and raise it from the reproduction of everyday things to the portrayal of loftier subjects in imitation of the painting of the period and which were not particularly related to the attributes of the new medium. The more orthodox of these artistic photographers wished to demonstrate that, like painting, the camera was capable of producing pictures of aesthetic merit, that the process responded to "handling" and that almost any current style in the painting of the day could be parallelled by photography. Rejlander explained, "I think that so far as the conception of a picture, the composition thereof, with the various expressions, and postures of the figures, the arrangements of draperies and costume, the distribution of light and shade and the preserving it, in one subordinate whole—that these various points which are essential in the production of a perfect picture, require the same operation of mind, the same artistic temperament and careful manipulation whether it be executed in crayon, paint or by a photographic agency".[45] At the first meeting of the new London Photographic Society, they claimed "photographs ought to be artistically, not chemically beautiful, a knowledge of the principles of art will enhance the photograph and most important, the object is better obtained by the whole subject being a little out of focus . . . more suggestive of the true character of nature".[46] This was the style in which Julia Margaret Cameron experimented. Diversely, those purists amongst the photographers insisted that the role of their medium was in allowing the photograph to achieve the state of art within its own properties; that photography contained the possibilities of its own aesthetic.

The imitation of painting gave way to gradual

27

28

awareness of the possibilities of transferring the aesthetics of painting to the photographic discipline and the growth of the "art" or "aesthetic" photograph. Although many argued, rightly, that the value in their work must be concerned with the elements of photography, nevertheless this manipulation of the process was still related to ideas of aesthetic possibilities exploited by painting; use of tone, asymetric composition, harmony, balance, graphic use of line, space, are still derived from the aesthetics of two-dimensional art although they now became expressed in photographic terms. This is not surprising since they projected the photograph as a two dimensional art object, a picture to be viewed within its individual context. They had arrived simply at a truth to materials. E. Durieu, President of the Société Française de Photographie, founded in Paris in November 1854, laid the foundation. "To call the brush to the aid of the photograph under the pretext of introducing art into it, is doing precisely the opposite—*excluding photographic art*". This doctrine which later became known as "straight photography" was developed in particular by Alfred Stieglitz (1864—1946) "by conviction and instinct an exponent of the 'straight photograph', working chiefly in the open air, with rapid exposures, leaving his models to pose themselves and relying for results upon means strictly photographic. He is to be counted among the Impressionists; fully conceiving his picture before he attempts to take it, seeking for effects of vivid actuality and reducing the final record to its simplest terms of expression".[47]

The importance of Stieglitz's work led to the present day art photographers such as Ansel Adams (b 1902), Cartier-Bresson (b 1908), Bill Brandt (b 1905) and Paul Strand (b 1890) who wrote "This objectivity is of the very essence of photography, its contribution and at the same time its limitation. The photographer's problem is to see clearly the limitations and at the same time the potential qualities of his medium, for it is precisely here that honesty no less than intensity of vision is the pre-requisite of a living expression.

This means a real respect for the thing in front of him expressed in terms of chiaroscuro . . . through a range of almost infinite tonal values which lie beyond the skill of human hand. The fullest realisation of this is accomplished without tricks of process or manipulation, through the use of straight photographic methods".[48] The photographer as artist had come of age, nevertheless they are still working within the tradition of the earliest art photographers.

The decision as to whether photography could be called art was finally reached in the famous case in the French courts in the years 1861-62, when Mayer and Pierson, who accused another team of photographers of pirating their prints of famous people, claimed the protection of the copyright laws. They did not realise that these applied only to the arts, consequently photography had first legally to be declared an art before it could be protected. A decision was finally reached and the court declared that it was an art. "Photographs could be the product of thought and spirit of taste and intelligence, and could bear the imprint of personality. Photographs could be art"[49] although a careful distinction was to be made between the artist photographer and the mechanist.[50] This was in spite of the fact that most artists of the day disagreed. Many artists who had become dependent on the photographic image could hardly declare that they were merely translating the photograph into paint.

These arguments of course implied a relationship to what was considered at that time as art. The implication being that the subject of photography did not exist; it was either art or merely a recording device and aid, or that the subject matter depicted was, of itself, the only importance. This confusion and simplification of photography's many values and functions is still problematic.

29

5. An Evaluation of the Photography of John Thomas

We have already seen how the photographer could express, in photographic terms through the manipulation of his medium, a personal aesthetic view of the world. In the beginning, photographers also realised, even if they did not fully understand, the power that lay in what we might describe as the "social" photograph. They soon learned that the photograph can have a powerful ability to arouse emotion and to make people more aware of a particular situation, as well as describe the world that surrounds them. Depending on *what* was taken and *how*, the photographer could recreate reality, or at least condition it, in order that the photograph contained a particular meaning or message. This has usually, but by no means exclusively been associated with social and political propaganda. Both these aspects of photography, although differing in intention, have considerable similarities; both are imposed manipulations of what we could define as the objective photograph, that is, the most objective reality the photograph is capable of rendering. The camera is an instrument which by its nature can record the most objective image we have yet been able to invent. It is our most perfect method of explaining the objective reality of the world in visual terms. It nevertheless conditions reality, in the same way that print processes and the use of drawn techniques prior to the invention of the photograph conditioned the nature of the translated representational image.[51]
At the one extreme we have the photograph which, although it records a situation does not have within its structure a sense of actuality of event; for the purpose of this definition we may call this the "descriptive" photograph. At the other extreme, we have the photograph which, through manipulation of the recording of the event contains a particular message or viewpoint. We have come to describe all of this section of photography as "documentary".[52] In this context we would call the photograph that contains actuality of event as nearer to the idea of documentary than the "descriptive" photograph or the "social comment". It is accepted that these three areas may well overlap.

Some early photographers recorded with great understanding the change taking place in their own locality, and were aware of the importance of photography as a documentary medium and within that context a propaganda tool, particularly in relation to the advocacy of social change. In the Mid-Victorian period, photographers did not, on the whole, concern themselves with social problems. Social conditions were not something to be looked at either with the naked eye or the camera (they were acceptable only as themes within art as long as they were suitably romanticised).

In 1877 Thomson began documenting the street life of London and Annan photographed the slums of Glasgow. This has been held to have marked a break through in photographic reporting and observation; more accurately defined as social comment for propaganda purposes. It is interesting to note that by 1877, John Thomas had already been established in this same tradition for ten years. Sutcliffe, by comparison, and with little interest in social comment for political purposes produced a social documentary of life at Whitby. Sutcliffe was an energetic and passionate photographer who had a deep admiration for the country and fisherfolk who earned their living from land and sea. His photographs, taken with delicacy and warmth, depict the strength, solemnity and humour of the people he loved, but they produce a personalised world, achieved by aesthetic and stylistic conventions that in time became "dated", romantic and inevitably sentimental simply because in our own time we have lost the necessity for that particular aesthetic imagery. In the same way, this applies to the outstanding photographs of life in East Anglia of P. H. Emerson (1856—1936). John Thomas' photographs are not in this category and must be assessed in a different light.

Few artists in the nineteenth century fully understood or utilised the fundamental attributes of the camera. They tried to imitate the painting of the day; to imbue the photograph with a sense of painterly logic. The

30

essential characteristic of the photograph is precisely its lack of pictorial logic. The inability of much of the work of the early photographers to identify the essential characteristics of the photograph (and in a sense our own inability) is understandable when one considers that all images prior to its invention were hand made or dependent on the syntax of the various printing processes which were conceived by human thought and manual skill. The camera, much as the early photographers and artists tried to deny or advocate its viability as a means of creating art objects is primarily a scientific instrument that is able to translate from the actual world and render an approximate image according to its own laws and according to its own logic. To the Victorians the camera was either capable of human control and hence expression as art or of little or no value. In the same way they regarded the processes of printmaking of value only as a means of reproducing as near as possible the art object (painting or sculpture) whereas in effect the print processes were the principal means of conveying visual information. "Thus the story of prints is not, as many people seem to think, that of a minor art form but that of a most powerful method of communication between men and of its effects upon western European thought and civilization".[53] This disregard is understandable since many of the new amateurs to photography lacked any form of art training and had never heard of any rules of composition and they tended to take rather free and easy snapshots. That position in photography is still present today.

John Thomas had no art training and it appeared was unaware of aesthetic considerations that occupied many of his contemporaries. He did not explore the wide pictorial possibilities of his medium, nor did he attempt to use the various modes of photographic creativity open to him. It must also be noted that the foundation of John Thomas' concept of photography was formulated prior to some of the photographers one is tempted to compare him with. The aesthetic appeal in a number of photographs may well be

accidental, they are imposed by the viewer rather than constructed through intention. At the time he was working the majority of photographers were too occupied with techniques and the majority of customers were too concerned with subject matter, not necessarily how it was depicted, to appreciate the aesthetic qualities of photography, particularly the pursuit of the photograph as an end in itself. It is only in recent years that developments in art have led to the investigation of aesthetics as an end in itself. Many of the early photographers currently being resurrected are praised not so much for content of message or even technical ability but simply for how the message is conveyed, since the audiences of today accept the notion of the photograph as an end in itself. We admire Sutcliffe not for what he is saying but the way he says it. This interpretation for the most part is imposed by our present art theory and not by the intentions of the photographer, although one could argue exceptions, for example the photography of Fox Talbot.

Whereas the aesthetic photographer perceives or imposes essential qualities of form and composition and interprets the scene or object according to those intentions, that is according to the notion of aesthetics of his day, in order to imbue the scene or object with his specific meaning, the documentary photographer at his most objective will attempt to simply reproduce and convey, not the experience, but the event. Both are limited to the degree of human imposition the science of photography allows. That degree in aesthetic terms, as P. H. Emerson was to find out was limited in relation to that of the painter. "But the all-vital power of selection and rejection are fatally limited, bound in by fixed and narrow barriers. No differential analysis can be made, no subduing of parts, save by dodging—no emphasis save by dodging, and that is not pure photography, impure photography is merely a confession of limitations . . . I thought once . . . that true values could be altered at will by development. They cannot, therefore, to talk of getting values in any subject whatever as you wish

31

and of getting them true to nature, is to talk nonsense . . . In short, I throw my lot in with those who say that photography is a very limited art. I deeply regret that I have come to this conclusion".[54] Emerson's comparison was in relation to the tradition of picture making and not an examination of the aesthetic possibilities peculiar to the photographic process itself. Unfortunately, to the majority of photographers there was no other comparison that could be made.

Clearly John Thomas was not in the tradition of Sutcliffe and Emerson, of the aesthetic or art photographer, for his photographs do not portray any awareness on his part for composition, form atmosphere, perspective, use of two-dimensional graphic space; more accurately, one is not aware of these elements as contributing factors in establishing meaning of statement. Photography is superior to all other arts in its extraordinary fine tonal gradation, from the brightest highlights to the deepest shadow and also its analysis and representation of form. There exists a number of possibilities; the choice of any subject, the choice of view point, camera angle, lighting, selection and elimination of detail, the stressing of one aspect of the subject as against another through differential focus, the choice of focal depth, the variations of the print through development, the gradation of the detail etc., all allow the photographer the latitude in interpretation and belie the idea of the straight objective photograph. However to take any kind of photograph requires some assessment and choice of these considerations. They are not unique to the aesthetic photographer. He is able to express within this photographic context both his own personality and/or his idea of the personality of his subject. Thomas' lack of knowledge of aesthetics and the fact that his motivation and intention were different, is evident. With no preconceived notions of composition, his arrangements of figures are unselective and, at times, as awkward as his subjects. The straggled group of farm workers at Carno Mill (Plate 23) displays no ability or conception of a balanced composition,

since there exists within the camera frame spacious areas of foreground and background within the setting. Again there seems no policy of planning in the hasty seating of the Capel Garmon Natives (Plate 39) at the corner of the street. The photographer seems unconscious of the potential of the exterior setting, if he had carefully positioned the group. Consequently, he has captured a cold stiff quality about the scene. Still further, he shows little awareness of the use of tonal qualities; textures, lights and shades, to impart any specific meaning to his subject matter. His photographs present few, if any, atmospherical qualities, but appear timeless and static. It was precisely this form of photography that William Lake Price argued against "what is most requisite is that the figures composing such groups would have an air of natural occupation, as if in their usual vocations or amusements. When heretofore, they have been attempted by amateurs and others, they have been shown as a stolid half circle of gaping figures intently staring at the lens".[55]

Sutcliffe, like Hill and Adamson, was able to retain a sense of immediacy of the moment, an interruption of time that captures an intimate impression. This immediacy and intimacy was essentially achieved by considered and careful *contrivance*. This is not to imply that Sutcliffe's photography is mere imitation of the painting of his day but it is achieved by similar means; it is within the same tradition and may be said to contain painterly qualities. Sutcliffe's sensitivity to space and atmosphere forced him to use extensive touching up procedures to further the quality of his photographs in order to achieve a greater degree of intention. His inclusion of mists and fog by means of tissue paper on the back of the plate negative showed the beauty that exists in the softness of a blurred image. It also demonstrates that whether the photograph is achieved through contrivance or not is immaterial, the fact that certain devices within the process are possible is also *photographic*. This distinction between "pure" and "impure" photography that Emerson noted was largely correct,

32

but of little consequence. It is particularly significant that he felt that the use of devices was wrong, unfortunately he seemed to be unable to see the logic and direction of the "pure" photographic statement.

The wet collodion's power of rendering detail, texture and form with marvellous clarity and exactitude and with comparable ease were considered its greatest merits. However, realising the use of all these elements and the potential of photography as an art medium takes the photographer into the realms of the artist. In so doing he must accept that the nature of the photograph is conditioned in order to allow this state to exist.

In the sphere of portrait photography, Thomas lacked the sensitive interpretations of Sutcliffe. By using his camera totally objectively on his subjects, Thomas was therefore unable or unwilling to project his own personality directly into his images, or project his notion of the personality of his sitters. His photographs of the country folk lack any indication of the photographer's compassion or emotion; they are 'abstract' statements; they are neither aesthetic, romantic nor social propaganda. For example, in the hasty arrangement of the Almshouse folk at Cerrigy-drudion (Plate 43), the figures are centralised within the camera frame, yet do not command the focal point. They appear insignificant, scared, lifeless, and Thomas has made no attempt at any form of social comment. This adds considerably to our appreciation of the photograph for we feel that he simply "took a photograph" and seems totally detached from the scene. The photograph is not a character analysis but simply a straightforward record and cannot be linked to the tradition of the painted portrait, on the contrary it is significantly a straightforward record of as near fact that the camera could convey. Why then is it such a powerful image?

Thomas' ignorance of the aesthetic norms of compositional form is also evident in these selected photographs, of scenes and persons (particularly Reverends) which have been mechanically "shot" one after another. Sutcliffe disliked the conventional strained forms of figure compositions and attempted to arrange them in as "natural" positions as possible, about their day-to-day work or in their normal settings. But Sutcliffe's attempts to produce "naturalism" or actuality nevertheless produce an idealised notion of subject matter as did Emersons. They are not "as they are" but as Sutcliffe "imagined them to be". Sutcliffe's constant feeling of dissatisfaction also drove him to treat each individual photograph separately to strive for the masterpiece. He only felt personally satisfied with a final finished print after long contemplation of the intended compositional form, accurate positioning of his subject matter and much alteration of the negative. Possibly a successful plate for John Thomas depended on whether it simply developed successfully. Sutcliffe's sense of failure in attempting to achieve a "perfect" photograph is nowhere found in Thomas' work, rather he used the camera to produce a mirror of reality which was, in his terms, the most real visual rendering in existence; he accepted the photograph, that is, the likeness that was possible, without contrivance, distortion, or conditioned aesthetics. He did not attempt to convey a personalised view of the world. Instead he took photographs as a record of "fact".

This comparison is also seen by an examination of intention and motivation; John Thomas was interested in depicting not only the famous people of his day but in providing a record of what he met on his travels. His motivation was primarily documentary and not photographic. Possibly in those isolated photographs which seem to have intentional aesthetic appeal this can be attributed rather to the unusualness of the subject matter, rather than the internal structure of the image. The photograph of Cemaes (Plate 2) clearly shows this.

His artistic talent in spite of the fact that he considered himself an artist, was severely limited. His

60

33

photographs however are appealing because they possess not only a kind of innocence and a lack of pretention, but also because they are striking images, rich in communication. They do hold an aesthetic appeal for our time in the very fact that the photographs contain neither emotional nor aesthetic content nor any artistic intention relative to his time; they are not locked in Victorian aesthetics or prejudices. Because of this absence, they have not become nostalgic nor sentimental, as have some of the work of his contemporaries. This aesthetic appeal however is distinct as it is imposed by our perception and not structured by the photographer's. Thomas, feeling he had a special "mission", considered himself over and above the realms of the ordinary street photographer and it is possible that but for this particular task which he set himself, and that Wales at that time was very poorly documented, he would have been one of the many Liverpool photographers and produced work of little importance. This was not the case and the fact that he cannot be considered as an art photographer need not necessarily detract from the value of his work. However in order to evaluate that contribution we need a definition of photography that is more meaningful than the one which continues to present all photography as merely differing degrees of aspiring to the condition called "art", particularly when that condition is within the tradition of art concepts related to the two-dimensional object as painted picture, and not to the distinctive logic and visual language of photography.

This distinction does not negate the work of the art photographers, on the contrary. However, the problem is that much current analysis of the early history of photography is in fact precisely orientated towards an evaluation of photographers as artists. Much of this historical analysis, like the photographers themselves, is derived from the discipline of art and art history and is not always helpful in an examination of photography *per se*. Much of this work still describes without distinction the activity of painting. While this is valid it does not

entirely explain or differentiate between other aspects of photography. We now seem to be able to accept the photographer as artist only in so far as he measures up to the idea of the creative painter. Sutcliffe proves that the photographer can be an artist in that sense, and the photograph a work of art, in so doing he proves that not all photography is art. But this does not imply that the non art photograph has no significance to our existence, to our understanding of reality.

John Thomas ambitiously worked to build up a collection of photographs which would form a lasting record of Wales and its inhabitants in the nineteenth century. He has made a record of the social groups of his time which only a camera could preserve. Thomas also realised that descriptive notes concerning the subject matter greatly enhanced the value of the images for posterity. Techniques have vastly changed and tastes in photographs altered, but this does not detract from the power of the image which he produced. This implies that a realistic examination of his kind of photograph lies outside the definition of the art photograph. Sutcliffe said "when you feel that a certain subject gives you pleasure you don't go to the trouble of analysing it and seeing whether the rules of art are properly exemplified, but you know that if you can with the aid of the camera reproduce on you plate these elements which please you, others will be pleased with the shadow you catch".[56] Although there is a certain truth in this, the distinction is of much more critical importance.

The particular characteristics of photographs such as these of John Thomas greatly enrich our historical awareness by allowing us to *see* as well as *know* our past. As William Lake Price commented "Posterity by the agency of photography will view the faithful image of our times, the future student in turning the page of history may at the same time look on the very eyes of those, long since mouldered to dust".[57] The stark imagery of some of Thomas' photographs are in this finest documentary tradition while many pre-date

34

35

63

these established by John Thomson and Thomas Annan. These photographs, static and timeless, devoid of device, precludes the historian's continual tendency to romanticise and fictionalise pre-photographic history. The sense of (photographic) actuality and its unselected social implications is a continual reminder of historical fiction. The visual image of the photograph is at least nearer "reality" that written make-believe. When confronted with some of John Thomas' photographs there is an overpowering sense of truth; one is aware of the social pattern of life in rural Wales, the poverty, dignity and character of the people in a way no written material can convey and in a way, by the very nature of the photograph, immediate and total, the description of the reality of the event cannot be adequately given in written form, nor do they require a written description to accompany them. "Seeing comes before words"[58] and "the image is more precise than literature".[59] We sense this when we look at the work of other photographers working now in this tradition. Donald McCullin (b 1935) springs to mind with his war photographs, which similarly we would not confuse with art. It is photographs such as these that have influenced contemporary man far more significantly than the art photographers; they are essentially nearer to the idea of a "pure" photography if in fact that term is appropriate at all. They are certainly more significant to our search for meaning and constitute the important images of our time.

The camera cannot be objective unless it is allowed to be; the absence of painterly activity, the absence of a personalised view of the world, of contrivance, brings us nearer in many respects to the photograph's essential potential and nearer to a definition of its characteristics. At their best, Thomas' photographs are far removed from the "snap-shot". This implies that there are degrees of documentary achievement, just as we accept degrees of aesthetic achievement. Whereas the argument has continually surrounded the necessity for individual manipulation of the photograph in order to allow aesthetic significance

"the photograph is the photographer",[60] and the justification for the photograph has been based on accepting this concept, the most difficult achievement in photography could well be said to be the production of totally objective photographic images. The image that signifies the reality of the object or scene without characteristics of period (that is, style), without imposed aesthetics, without imposed political or social comment and propaganda, without imposing the individuality of the photographer, that contains a sense of actuality, and at the same time is concerned with photographic language, which is not a substitute for the image itself, is extremely rare. These photographs are distinct from the millions of largely meaningless descriptive photography that surrounds us. It is perhaps because of the quantity of descriptive photography that we have lost sight of the importance of the documentary objective photograph. Nevertheless it should not be forgotten that the snap-shots of one's friends on holiday, staring at the camera lens depicts the *real* situation of *that* event i.e taking that particular photograph; rather than the professional, contrived, extremely aesthetic but meaningless advertisement photograph that masquerades as a standard of photographic excellence.

Indeed if one examines photography as used in current advertising we see the logical end result of art photography, one can immediately see the absurdity of the predominant concept of the photographer as artist. Our inability to differentiate sufficiently between the two areas explains our acceptance of Donald McCullin's harrowing photographs of war victims, or the starving children of the world side by side with the total artificiality of the publicity dream. An examination of the work of John Thomas interrupts that happy coexistence and poses a fundamental difference and distinction. "It is a mistake to think of publicity supplanting the visual art of post-Renaissance Europe; it is the last moribund form of that art".[61] Clearly photography used for advertising and publicity is structured

36

through similar patterns to the art photograph. This is understandable when one considers that photographers are trained fundamentally in the same way and within the same context as artists. Although the advertising photograph has different intentions and meaning, and constitutes the totally contrived and artificial photograph in an attempt to signify reality, it is the most unreal form of photography possible. It is significant of our society that the most accomplished aesthetic and technical photography of our time has been completely disassociated from reality and experience, from the basic characteristics of the camera and its most forceful attribute.

If we believe that the "experience of seeking (is) to give meaning to our lives, of trying to understand the history of which we can become the active agents"[62] then John Thomas' work is highly significant. Their value is precisely because they record in a highly objective manner, without hindrance even from social or political comment, they record the reality of his time with considerable sense of actuality. Their simplicity of statement is their virtue and achievement. We achieve this uninterrupted reading and thus a greater awareness not only of his reality but also of our own. "We never look at just one thing; we are always looking at the relation between things and ourselves".[63]

John Thomas' work, although differing in intention, has marked similarities with Fox Talbot, the father of photography and perhaps the most undervalued photographer. It is significant (particularly within the context of this study) that there has been little investigation and response into the relevance of Talbot's photographs; these have been neglected in preference to the study of his inventions and the scientific contribution to photography which gave us the positive/negative multiple image, in fact gave us the photograph as we know it. Unfortunately a great deal of the significance of his work has become obscured with out preoccupation with subsequent presentations. There is more than ever the need for a

major study of his work. There are similarities between Talbot and some of Thomas' work and in attempting any definition of photography one is inevitably drawn back to Talbot's use of the camera, particularly in his prime investigation of what constitutes the *photographic*. "The point about Talbot's work, of course, is that it declares itself as artefact. The unmistakeable subject of most of his calotypes is nothing more than the photograph itself as a means of representing".[64]

To some extent we could also say this of many of Thomas' photographs, but whereas Talbot's work is primarily concerned with this investigation of the means of representing that in turn defines the photographic process and establishes the alphabet of photographic language, Thomas has, in accepting them, simply, but significantly, added the notion of importance of specific subject matter. That is not the use of subject matter controlled to explain the photographic image as in Talbot's case, but using the notion of the photographic image as artefact certainly, but principally as a vehicle to hold subject matter, by so doing, the statement becomes the photograph itself and subsequent meaning is additional and invented by the viewer. In spite of the stiff pose, the arbitrary composition, these photographs are alive and powerful in a way that much social documentary photography for effect, albeit well motivated, is not and thus they become the more objective photography and the more valuable one. If one accepts a definition of degrees of documentary which is also distinct from art, then his work is within the finest documentary reportage tradition.

The existence of the collection of over 3000 negatives makes his contribution of major importance. His work ranks with several of his more famous contemporaries who have recently achieved recognition.

Each new art theory increases our awareness of the present and inevitably our perception of the past to the extent that former works take on the nature of the

37

theory and become relevant to the present and to our realisation of our existence. John Thomas set out with the simple intention of recording his society and his landscape which could only be achieved after the end of his collection. He did not strive for the individual photograph but searched for the collective. His photography is representative of the collective consciousness of his society rather than the exaltation of the individual as artist and in achieving this, he develops similar characteristics to current conceptual and idea art. Within that context, John Thomas could well be said to be an artist of particular significance for our time, since "things are because we see them, and what we see, and how we see it, depends on the arts that have influenced us".[65] Wherever he may eventually be placed in the early history of photography there is little doubt that some of his striking images will become our truest definition of life in late nineteenth century Wales. In so doing, this is perhaps the greatest contribution photography can make to society.

38

Notes and References to the Text

NATURE OF THE SOURCES

The most useful material is to be found in the two articles by Dr. Emyr Wyn Jones printed in the *Journal of the Merioneth Historical and Record Society (1963)*, vol iv, no iii, pp 242-273 entitled *"John Thomas, Cambrian Gallery: Ei Atgofion a'i Deithiau"* and an article in the *Journal of the National Library of Wales (1956)* vol ix, no 4. These include the only published passages and extracts from John Thomas' memoirs as well as details from other family documents and letters.

There exists no other direct reference to John Thomas, except in the Dictionary of Welsh Biography under his son William Thelwall Thomas.

E. D. Jones also acknowledges the use of many photographs from the John Thomas Collection, which illustrates his recent book, *"Victorian and Edwardian Wales"*.

All unacknowledged quotations in the text have been taken from the article by Dr. Emyr Wyn Jones, in the Journal of the Merioneth Historical and Record Society (1963), who in turn selected material from the notebooks of John Thomas.

1 *College by the Sea 1928*, J. Ballinger, The National Library of Wales. II
2 Details given by Anne Roberts the great grand-daughter of John Thomas.
3 *Journal of the National Library of Wales,* Winter 1956. Vol. IX. No. 4. "John Thomas of the Cambrian Gallery" by Dr. Emyr Wyn Jones, p. 385.
4 Jane Thomas died in 1870 and was buried in the family graveyard in Cellan.
5 These are in the form of seven books in good handwriting covering reminiscences over a period of forty years. The author starts very methodically by writing on the cover of the first book "Written by John Thomas, Cambrian Gallery, Liverpool at Abersilio, near Llangollen, Oct. 4th, 1904" (he had also a branch of his business at Llangollen for many years). Then he adds a subtitle "Also the travels of John Thomas (Cambrian Gallery) through the whole of Wales". John Thomas' main aim in writing would appear to be in order to give additional information to those who purchased his photographs. At the top of the first page of the exercise books he wrote, "The story of the setting up of the Cambrian Gallery, Liverpool or (the Welsh Gallery)". Passages from these autobiographical writings and other information has been acquired from that which Dr. Wyn Jones directly selected from the notebooks for his article in the *Journal of the Merioneth Historical and Record Society (1963) Vol. IV. No. III. pp. 242-273*. The original notebooks lie in the keeping of Dr. Ifor Davies, of Moelwyn, Cerrigydrudion, John Thomas' grand-daughter's husband.
6 Llewelyn Ap Iorwerth (1194-1246) or Llywelyn Fawr (the Great) was the Prince of Gwynedd and won himself the overlordship of all Wales under vassalage to the English throne. He married Johanna the daughter of King John.
7 A name which photography earned by the fact that its chemicals often blackened the hands and clothes of its early devotees.
8 Harry Emmens was a "photographic artist" whose name appeared for the first time in the Liverpool Directory in 1864. He operated as a photographer in various places in the city during the next ten years. From 1874-76 his name appears as Director of Brougham Terrace Social Club, West Derby Road, Liverpool.
9 The name "Cambrian Gallery" did last forty years in spite of several changes of address as the business expanded: from 66, St Anne St., then to 47, Everton Road and finally to 68, Queen's Road (as the *Liverpool Directory* records) until it was renamed "Yr Oriel Cymraeg" (The Welsh Gallery) when the business came into the hands of (Sir) O. M. Edwards (see 10). A branch of the business also existed for many years in Regent Street, Llangollen.
10 Reference to O. M. Edwards (later Sir O. M. Edwards) 1858-1920 in the *Dictionary of Welsh Biography* describes him as a prolific writer and lover of the Welsh language. He is mentioned as intended for the Ministry, but studied at University College of Wales, Aberystwyth, later at Oxford where he reverted to history and had a brilliant career, teaching at Oxford from 1889 to 1907. Most of his books and articles on the history of Wales were published in Welsh. He frequently used Thomas' photographs in these as illustrations and also in the many articles he wrote. In 1890 he was co-editor of 'Cymru Fydd' but by 1891 he was publishing the periodical 'Cymru' on his own account. O. M. Edwards' son, Sir Ifan ab Owen Edwards 1895-1970, who had an equally distinguished

39

career, donated his father's collections to the National Library of Wales in 1930.

11 op. cit. (3) p. 390.

12 Helmut Gernsheim *Creative Photography, Aesthetic Trends 1839 to Modern Times,* Faber and Faber 1962.

13 Michael Hiley *"Frank Meadow Sutcliffe, Photographer of Whitby".* Gordon Fraser Photographic Monographs: 1 1974.

14 The "carte-de visite" photograph at first intended to supplement visiting cards, was popularised by André Adolphe Disderi of Paris in 1859, although the idea seems to have been thought of independently in many countries. Controversy exists as to who exactly is responsible for the invention of the carte-de-visite. The craze soon spread to England and in the 1860's several hundred million of them were sold. It became the custom to exchange "cartes" with friends. Although they were made up to about 1880 their popularity began to wane after about 1866. They were usually a full length portrait mounted on a card measuring about 4″ x 2½″ and were the standard small size for portrait photographs.

15 Certain sixteenth century paintings show a similar incongruity of middle class sitters in palatial decor or with obviously unsuitable accessories. Some of the Dutch merchants painted by Frans Hals were pompously posed in aristocratic attire in front of imaginary palatial backgrounds . . . this was only a pictorial revival of the age-old desire to appear more important than one really is.

16 Valerie Lloyd *"The Camera and Doctor Barnardo"* (Introduction by Gilliam Wagner), Barnardo School of Printing, Hertfordshire.

17 With the old system on glass, there would have been a reversion of the image but with the negative positive process which John Thomas used the printing reversed it back, so that the print appeared the correct way round.

18 The Art Journal 1859, p. 71.

19 "Vignetting", a term referring to the softening of edges with the use of such things as cardboard masks, blocking out with black varnish or sprays to wash away pigmented photo-sensitised gelatine.

20 "retouching", was first used c. 1865-70. It was possible to retouch both wet and dry plate negatives whether portrait, landscape or any other subject. The black lead pencil first came to be used to correct the faulty colour rendering of plates used for portraiture. The procedure was as described by F. M. Sutcliffe.

"The negative was varnished, a necessary precaution then to keep the collodion film from peeling off the plate; then the face of the varnish over the features was made dull by rubbing it over with powdered bath brick or cuttlefish powder till it was rough enough to take to the pencil. Then the retoucher set to work. In the end he generally made the victim, whether male or female more like a bladder of lard than a human being when he had finished the plate." (5 December 1925). M. Hiley "Frank Sutcliffe, Photographer of Whitby". p. 141.

21 op. cit. (17).

22 Although Niépce is given the credit of having devised the first photographic process and of having invented the earliest photographing method, Daguerre can be credited with having made photography "practical" as distinct from "possible". From 1839 to 1857 the "Daguerreotype" was in general use.

23 In c. 1853 Talbot had put forward the claim that collodion was covered by his calotype patent and therefore issued injunctions against many English photographers.

24 Helmut and Alison Gernsheim *"The History of Photography"* Thames and Hudson 1955 p. 239.

25 "The Photographic News", Aug. 1861, p. 370.

26 The average photographer would try to make his sitter's features conform to the Victorian ideal of beauty. "The colourist", ran one instruction, "may correct with his brush defects which if allowed to remain, spoil any picture, for instance where a head is so irregular in form as to become unsightly, soften those features, which are, the most strikingly deformed, and reduce the head to a greater semblance of beauty. Try to discover what good points there are and give these their full value". The Photographic News, 3 June 1859, p. 149.

27 op. cit (24), p. 234.

28 This technique developed into combination printing, a form of photomontage involving the arrangement of several negatives which were then printed to produce composed pictures which often resembled Victorian narrative painting.

29 Aaron Scharf *"Art and Photography"* Pelican (Revised edition, 1974, p. 114).
30 op. cit (13), p. 59.
31 *"From Today Painting is Dead"*. *The Beginnings of Photography*. The Arts Council of Great Britain. Victoria and Albert Museum, p. 7.
32 F. M. Sutcliffe, *"To Parents and Guardians"*, Amateur Photography, 12 July 1901, p. 31-2.
33 c.f. Preface of G. Ovenden's *"Julia Margaret Cameron, Victorian Photographer of Fair Men and Women"*, Hogarth Press.
34 op. cit (29), p. 320.
35 G. M. Trevelyan, *"English Social History"*, Vol. IV, p. 57.
36 M. A. Root, *"The Camera and the Pencil"* (New York, 1864),
37 op. cit (35), p. 571 (Reprint from The Photographic News, London, 1861, p. 500).
38 op. cit (31), Tristram Powell, *"Fixing the Face"*, p. 9.
39 op. cit (38).
40 Baudelaire. *"Review of the Salon of 1859"* reprinted in Gernsheim's "History of Photography".
41 Poynter. *"Ten Lectures on Art"*, 1879. London. See pp. 38, 190.
42 Reprint from P. H. Emerson *"Naturalistic Photography"*, London, 1889, p. 282.
43 op. cit (29), p. 353.
44 F. M. Sutcliffe. From Rev. C. Lambert's *"The Pictorial Work of Frank M. Sutcliffe"*, The Practical Photographer, No. 8, May 1904, pp. 2-3.
45 The Photographic Journal, 21 April, 1858.
46 Newton, *"Upon Photography in an Artistic View and its Relations to the Arts"*, Photographic Society Journal. June 1853, p. 67.
47 Charles Caffin on Arthur Steiglitz. Beaumont Newhall, *The History of Photography*, 1964, p. 111.
48 P. Strand, *Camera Work Nos. 49-50*, June 1917.
49 op. cit (29), p. 153.
50 In 1859 the French Government had finally yielded to the pressure of the Société Française de Photographie and its supporters. Authorised by the Minister of State and the Imperial Director of Fine Arts, a Salon of Photography formed part of the yearly exhibitions held in the Palais de l' Industrie. Nadar probably was the most effective force in engineering photography's new triumph.
51 William M. Irvins, *"Prints and Visual Communication"*, the MIT Press, 1953.
52 The term *documentary* was first coined by John Grierson (1898-1972) in 1929 when he founded a school of "documentarists" who believed in making films about real life as distinct from studio fiction, although several films in this category had been made prior to Grierson's "The Drifters", notably Flaherty's "Nanook of the North". Grierson believed that reality could be changed by the artist into powerful social, educational, political propaganda and his films have to an extent the same characteristics as Sutcliffe's photographs. The definition of "Documentary" used in this study, however, would include Grierson's only as one area.
53 op. cit, 51.
54 P. H. Emerson, *The Death of Naturalistic Photography*, 1891 (see 47).
55 William Lake Price, *"A Manual of Photographic Manipulation Treating of the Practice of the Art and its various applications to Nature"*, London, 1868, pp. 4-6.
56 F. M. Sutcliffe, *"Art and Photography"*, Photography, 7 May 1891, p. 290.
57 op. cit (55).
58 John Berger, *Ways of Seeing*, Pelican, 1972.
59 ibid. (58).
60 Henri Cartier-Bresson, b. 1908.
61 op. cit (58).
62 ibid. (58).
63 ibid. (58).
64 Ian Jeffrey, *The Real Thing*, exhibition c catalogue, The Arts Council of Great Britain, 1975.
65 Oscar Wilde, *Intentions*, London, 1891.

41

Bibliography

Ackerman, C. W.	"*George Eastman*", Boston: Houghton Mifflin 1930.	Gernsheim, H.	"*L. J. M. Daguerre, the history of the diorama and daguerreotype*" London 1956
Berger, J.	"*Ways of Seeing*" Pelican 1972	,,	"*Creative Photography: 1826 to the Present: From the Gernsheim Collection*" Wayne St. Un. Press 1963
Braive, M. F.	"*The Era of the Photograph*" Thames and Hudson, 1969	,,	"*Julia Margaret Cameron*" An Aperture Monograph, 1974
Buckland, G.	"*Reality Recorded*". Early Documentary Photography David and Charles, 1974	,,	"*Lewis Carroll, Photographer*" Peter Smith 1949
Coe, B.	"*George Eastman and the Early Photographers*" (Pioneers of Science and Discovery), London 1973	,,	"*Creative Photography: Aesthetic Trends 1839 to Modern Times*" Faber and Faber 1962
Coke, Van Deren	"*The Painter and the Photograph*" University of New Mexico Press 1964	Hiley, M.	"*Frank Sutcliffe, Photographer of Whitby*" Gordon Fraser Photographic Monographs: 1 1974
Eastman, G.	"*A book about portrait film. By the men who use it*" London 1921	Grey, H. and Stuart, G.	"*The Victorian at Sea*" St. Martin. Academy Photographic Editions 1973
Evans, H. and M.	"*The Victorians: At Home and At Work as Illustrated by Themselves*" Arco. 1973	Howarth-Loomes, B. F. C.	"*Victorian Photography, a collector's guide*" Ward Lock, London 1974
Ford, C. and Strong, R.	"*The Hill and Adamson Collection: An Early Victorian Album*" 1974	Jones, E.	"*Father of Art Photography: O. J. Rejlander 1813-1875*" David and Charles 1974
Grensheim, H. and A.	"*The History of Photography*" Thames and Hudson 1955 and revised edition 1969	Jones, E. D.	"*Victorian and Edwardian Wales*" B. T. Batsford Ltd. 1972
Gernsheim, H. and A.	"*A Concise History of Photography*" Thames and Hudson (revised edition, 1971)	Lloyd, V.	"*The Camera and Dr. Barnardo*" Barnardo School of Printing, Hertfordshire

76

42

Moholy, L.	*"A Hundred Years of Photography"* Penguin 1939	Winter, G.	*"Country Camera, 1844-1914: Rural Life as Depicted in Photographs from the Early Days of Photography to the Outbreak of the First World War"* Gale 1971
Newhall, B.	*"The History of Photography"* New York, 1964		
Ovenden, G.	*"Pre-Raphaelite Photography"* St. Martin Academy Photographic Editions 1972	,,	*"Past Positives: London's Social History Recorded in Photographs"* Intl. Pubrs. Serv.
,,	*"Julia Margaret Cameron: Victorian Photographer of Fair Men and Women"* Hogarth Press	,,	*"A Country Camera"* Penguin 1974
,,	*"David Octavius Hill and Robert Adamson"* St. Martin 1974		
Ovenden, G. and Melville, R.	*"Victorian Children"* St. Martin Photographic Editions 1972		
Scharf, A.	*"Art and Photography"* Pelican (revised edition 1974)		
Staley, A.	*"The Pre-Raphaelite Landscape"* Oxford Studies in the History of Art and Architecture Oxford University Press 1973		
Thomas, D. B.	*"The First Negatives"* H.M.S.O 1964		
,,	*"Cameras"* H.M.S.O. 1968		
Trevelyan, G. M.	*"English Social History"* Vol. IV. The Nineteenth Century, McKay 1949-52		
Wall, A. H.	*"Artistic Landscape Photography"*. The Lit. of Photography Ser. 1896		

43

Exhibition Catalogues

"From Today Painting is Dead", The Beginnings of
Photography
An exhibition held at the Victoria and Albert Museum,
London, 16 March—14 May 1972.

Master pieces of Victorian Photographers 1840—1900
From the Gernsheim Collection an exhibition at the
Victoria and Albert Museum, London, 1 May—11 October
1951

David Octavius Hill 1892—1870, Robert Adamson
1821—1848
An exhibition arranged by the Scottish Arts Council 1970.

The Camera goes to War, photographs from the Crimean
War 1854-56
An exhibition arranged by the Scottish Arts Council 1974.

The Real Thing
An exhibition arranged by the Arts Council of Great Britain
1975.

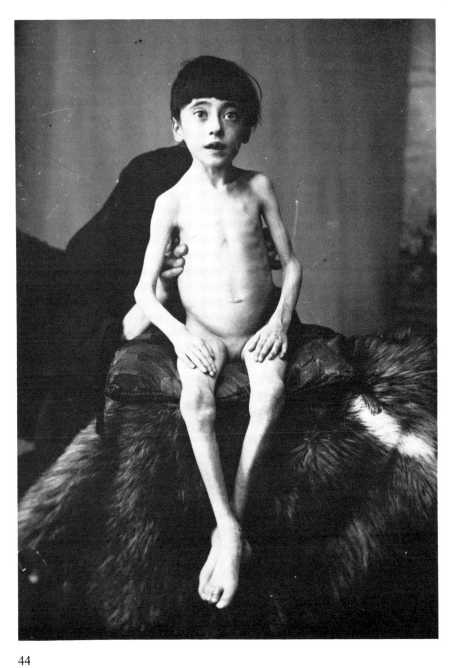

44